WILD
INDIANS

WILD
INDIANS

and
Oher Common Misconceptions:

A Real Life
on the
Mission Field

Carol Martin

 **VMI** PUBLISHERS

Partnering With Christian Authors, Publishing Christian and Inspirational Books

Sister, Oregon

Published by
VMI Publishers
Sisters, Oregon
www.vmipublishers.com

ISBN: 1-933204-42-7
ISBN 13: 978-1-933204-42-0

Library of Congress Control Number: 2007933439

Printed in the USA.

Cover design by Joe Bailen

This book is dedicated to Chasyti, Colton, Mitchell,
Rickey, Jessica, Titus, and Moren.
It is my prayer that you grow to love and embrace Jesus
as Lord and Savior and walk with Him closely all your days.

CONTENTS

1

THE TIME OF CHILDHOOD

*"There is a time for everything,
and a season for every activity under heaven."*
ECCLESIASTES 3:1

January 23, 1945 was a very cold morning in Big Rapids,
Michigan. It had snowed during the night, covering the ground
with a fresh blanket. As the dawn broke, most of the residents were just
beginning to stir. Not so with my mother. She had been laboring most of
the night, for this interesting date of 01/23/45 was about to become my
birthday.

Beside her sat my grandmother. My grandparents, Byron and Nellie
Hahn, lived in a parsonage. Grandpa was a Methodist minister, and be-
cause of that, Mother and her siblings had to move from town to town,
the prevailing thought being that after a few years, a minister lost his ef-
fectiveness, so on to another church. New schools, new friends, and new
surroundings, however, were not the only hardships. The family was poor
and what little they had was often shared with church members who had
even less.

We left the hospital when I was five days old and moved into the
parsonage. My sister, Kay, my mother, and I lived with my grandparents.
My father was in the army and I wouldn't meet him for nine months.

Soon after he got out of the army, we moved to Alma, Michigan, where we lived until I was fifteen. My other grandparents, Harold and Clara Redman, also lived in Alma.

Dad drove a grocery truck for a warehouse. We were rather poor, but I didn't notice. These were happy years. My grandparents were good friends. They loved to go into the Upper Peninsula or Canada to go fishing together. Grandpa Redman built a very small trailer for them to sleep in and carry their stuff. He put wheels on it and they towed this to the UP and Canada. Many of his neighbors wanted a "travel trailer" like this, so Grandpa began building trailers for his neighbors. These were very popular. As these neighbors went camping, other people saw the trailers; they wanted a trailer too. Soon Grandpa had so many orders he had to hire others, including my dad, to help him build trailers. Within a few years, he had a factory and was building larger and larger trailers. He called his new company New Moon Homes. He retired in his midfifties to hunt, fish, and garden and my dad, at twenty-eight, took over the company. Under Dad's management, this one plant grew to more than thirty factories located all over the U.S. In 1960, Dad moved the corporate office to Dallas, Texas. I was in high school, and this was very traumatic for me—but I'm getting ahead of myself.

Making these trailers meant making more money for my dad, and by the time I was seven, we had moved into one of the biggest houses in Alma. We also had a trailer on a little lot at Higgins Lake. We spent our summers at the lake, swimming, skiing, and sailing. Dad got his pilot's license, bought a small plane, and flew the sixty-plus mile commute from Higgins Lake to Alma each day. He would buzz overhead and we would all hop in the car and drive over to the Houghton Lake airport to pick him up.

My parents soon sold the trailer and upgraded to a cottage; by then, Mary, Jon, and Janey had arrived in our family, so now we were seven. My cousins would come to the lake and spend two weeks every summer. What fun we had! We learned to swim, water-ski, sail, and paddle a canoe. Michigan has cold days, even in summer, and on these cold, wet days, Kay and I would build a fire on the beach and pretend we were shipwrecked. If it was too rainy, we would play canasta inside, often making so much noise we woke up baby Janey, who was colicky for months.

Labor Day meant the end of summer and leaving Higgins Lake. After winterizing the cottage, we would go to Chicago to buy school clothes. The autumns in Michigan were beautiful with brilliant colors. They were also short, and winter came quickly. Daylight occurred while we were in school; we went to school in the dark and came home in the dark. We loved the winters, and we loved our winter activities. We had a huge hill at the side of our house, and as soon as snow covered it, most of the neighborhood kids came over to slide down our hill. We slid down on a variety of vehicles, like cardboard boxes and garbage can lids. Kay and I had best friends, Kathy and Kristy McClure, who lived just three houses down the road. Their dad made an ice skating rink each winter. The rink was equipped with lights and music, so after supper, we all gathered there to skate. We learned to snow ski at a very early age. I don't remember learning to ski, just as I don't remember learning to walk.

I grew up attending the First United Methodist Church. My Uncle Charlie was the minister. Dad taught Sunday school and Mom sang in the choir. When I was in junior high, I too sang in the choir. We were the model Christian family. Dad offered Kay and me fifty dollars to memorize the Sermon on the Mount, which was a favorite passage of his. We managed to memorize most of it, but not the whole passage, so we never collected the prize. I'm grateful for this upbringing, this early training. I never questioned the existence of God. From my earliest memories, I was taught that God created the earth and all living things, and this made sense to me. I could see His hand all around me, the Heavens declaring His handiwork. We were also taught to do good, to be good. This was how we pleased God. A personal relationship with Jesus wasn't discussed. I saw the Christian life as a scale of justice. On one side were our good works and on the opposite side were our bad deeds. When you died, all deeds were tallied up and you were given your score. Good luck.

I somehow knew that I would never be good enough. I might be able to look good enough, being beneficent, gracious, and content, while secretly harboring critical, contemptible thoughts of others. I was jealous when I came in second when running for student council president. I enjoyed getting better grades than most of my friends. I enjoyed the fact that my dad had an airplane and was a pilot, and that we had a summer cottage. The list went on. I wanted good for others, just so long as I did a little better, had a little more. This made me feel good about myself. No amount of good deeds, however, could outweigh my petty jealousies, my self-righteous, critical attitudes, or my pride in the scale of justice. By the time I was in college, I knew I didn't stand a chance in hell to make it to heaven. But I'm getting ahead of myself again.

2

AN EARNEST PLEA

"Hear, O Lord, my righteous plea;
listen to my cry. Give ear to my prayer."
PSALM 17:1

*W*hen I was fifteen, we moved to Dallas. We had not moved since we were a family of four and now we numbered seven and as with most families, we had accumulated volumes of stuff. We all helped Mother pack. When a box was full, taped shut, and labeled, it was put into a room newly designated to store these boxes. This room gradually began to fill up, while the rest of the house began to look bare. Finally, the big day came. The movers arrived and first removed all the furniture, then all the boxes. With tears streaming down my face, I walked through this beautiful old house where I had spent my happy childhood years. I felt as desolate as the rooms looked. My life was ruined. Would I ever be happy again? I didn't think so. A bit dramatic, I admit, but remember, I was fifteen.

The movers were scheduled to take six days to get to Texas. During that time, we all moved over to Grandma and Grandpa Redman's house. They had a small, two-bedroom house, but they were on vacation, so we had the house all to ourselves. Kay and I slept in the family room on pallets on the floor and tried to convince ourselves it was a slumber party. My grandparents had several jigsaw puzzles. Since we were bored almost to the point of inertia, we decided to put together all the puzzles they owned. Now we had a challenge, a goal. This made the days fly past and by the time my grandparents returned home, every flat surface in their house was covered with a puzzle, every piece in place.

On the fourth day, we headed to the airport. We were on our way to our new home. We landed at the Dallas Love Field Airport. When I walk into this terminal now it seems rather small, but in 1960, to a small town gal, it was huge and fascinating. Dad ran ahead to check on our luggage, while Mother and her brood of five trailed behind. Kay and I were stopping to stare at people and soon lagged way behind. As we entered the main lobby, Kay looked up to the high ceiling and tripped. She grabbed my arm as she fell and I toppled on top of her. Thus, our grand entrance into Big D began and ended with us sprawled out on the floor of the airport. Mother turned to make sure we were still following just in time to see a policeman rush up to us to help us to our feet. She was so embarrassed; she didn't even stop or acknowledge she knew us. She just kept walking. Kay and I were mortified beyond description and began giggling uncontrollably.

We were still having periodic outbursts of snickers as we pulled away from Love Field in two separate taxis. We spent the next couple of nights at a Holiday Inn close to our new home. The house was large and beautiful and we unpacked and settled in quickly.

This move from a little town where we knew almost everyone to being plunked down in cosmopolitan Dallas was a tremendous shock for all of us. Kay was a senior and I was a sophomore. That first year, we never really did fit in and were pretty much misfits. Each day we would come home and cry. Mom would make coffee and we would drink coffee, eat cookies, and cry. Some days, Mom would ask us to find just one good thing about our new school. That was hard. We missed our friends. We were miserable.

Reflecting on this time as an adult, I now realize that my mother was also a misfit. Being raised in near poverty didn't prepare her for this thriving metropolis, this center of fashion. From hand-me-downs to Neiman Marcus, Mother had come a long way. She, too, was striving to be accepted.

Much of Dallas was oozing with wealth. Kids my age were driving the latest cars. We met our neighbors and their five-year-old daughter showed us her new Christian Dior dress. What, I wondered, was a Christian Dior dress? It looked like any other dress to my unsophisticated eyes. But soon we joined the throngs traveling the loop of the materialistic highway on our way to buy more, have more, wear the latest, drive the best, and eat at the newest hot spots. I call this the loop because it buys no satisfaction, brings no lasting joy, and, in truth, goes nowhere. At fifteen, I didn't understand the futility of this insatiable path and thus in my desire to fit in, I climbed on wholeheartedly, becoming a snob in my own right. Dad hadn't become wealthy overnight, but almost, and we quickly embraced the perks reserved for those who have.

Within a few years, the simple, contented lifestyle of Alma was a distant memory. The true friendships of my youth were replaced with hanging out with people who impressed me and I them. I was still lonely, but at least, now, I fit in.

For years, my mother had been busy raising three younger siblings. Now her schedule also included making a place in Dallas. This wasn't a big problem for me, as it was my father, not my mother, who had always been the nurturing parent. He was the one who taught me to ice skate, water-ski, and ride a bike. He was the one who read bedtime stories to Kay and me. He was the one who helped me with my homework. On long walks in the snow, or down railroad tracks, he spoke to me about honesty, integrity, and the importance of goals and achievements.

My work ethic and sense of humor came from my dad. If I wanted to talk, he was always there. All this changed with the move to Dallas. He worked longer hours. This combined with the longer commute meant that he wasn't home near as often as he previously had been. He no longer had time for me. I missed the special times we had shared, but had discovered boys, and soon this void was filled with one boyfriend after another. I was needy and looking for affection; they were all too happy to oblige me. I became giddy with all the attention. My schoolwork suffered. My father was quick to notice and began telling me I was heading in the wrong direction, heading for the gutter. I ignored his advice, and he lacked the time to guide me. There may be young teenagers responsible enough to manage their own lives, but unfortunately, I wasn't one of them. I quickly learned to give my parents lip service while doing my own thing behind their backs. I often sneaked out of the house after bedtime, carousing around with my latest boyfriend. I was fortunate these two years of unrestricted activity didn't result in life changing consequences.

Kay had gone to Texas Tech and two years later, I followed. My parents, being too busy working and socializing, sent Jack Henry, the company pilot, to accompany me to college. I had known Jack for many years and he was a very nice man, but as he helped me move into the dorm and I watched all my classmates with their parents, hugging and kissing them good-bye, I vowed I would never *send* my children to college, I would *take* them. I would help them move in. I would hug and kiss them good-bye. I shook Jack's hand and felt very much alone.

But I still had Kay. By this time, she had met and married Roger Chafin and they lived in Lubbock. Kay and I often said that we raised each other. So now, not only Kay, but Roger, too, became my surrogate parent. This was a job they didn't ask for or desire, but they did their best. More than once, having missed curfew and being locked out of the dorm, I would bang on their door, waking them up from a sound sleep, asking to spend the night once again on their couch.

One evening I went to a fraternity party. Dan, my date, was cute and lots of fun. I could see he was well liked among his friends and I was having a great time, laughing and drinking. It did seem like Dan was drinking more than his share, but what the heck. Around midnight, I told him I needed to get back to the dorm. We left and staggered to the car. He helped me into my side like a gentleman. When he was in the car, he leaned across me and said, "I want to show you something." He opened the glove compartment and pulled out a gun! He aimed it at my chest and I pushed his arm away just as the gun went off and a bullet went into the passenger door just in front of me. The firing of the gun shocked him almost as much as me. I had never been so scared in my life and started yelling that I wanted to go home immediately. He took off down the street and turned left at the first intersection. As it turned out, this wasn't an intersection, but a railroad track. In his inebriated state, he didn't seem to realize that we were now bouncing down a railroad track. I was still reeling from the gunshot but did notice that a very bright light was heading in our direction and was getting larger with each moment. To my horror, I quickly realized it was a train bearing down on us. I yelled for Dan to get off the track. He nonchalantly kept driving down the tracks, the car bouncing wildly. I grabbed the steering wheel and he shoved me away. In panic, I hopped into the backseat and hid on the floor. This was stupid. I then hopped back into the front seat. My adrenaline was running at an all time high and I hit him in the head, knocking him out cold. I grabbed the steering wheel, gunned the motor, and jerked the car off the track, causing it to careen down a very steep embankment.

I heard the train roar past far above us. The car came to a sudden halt as it rammed into a telephone pole at the bottom, pinning the passenger door shut. The car leaned precariously at a forty-five degree angle, the telephone pole preventing the complete rollover. I had a large, painful, bruise on my forehead. Dan was still unconscious. I again climbed into the back seat, managed to push open the door behind the driver's seat, pulled myself out of the car, and crawled up to the tracks. I began walking back to where I thought we had started. I hadn't been walking long before I heard Dan calling my name behind me. I began to run as fast as I could, tripping over the trestles. I had visions of him chasing after me with his gun.

I turned onto a street as soon as I could and found myself wandering in an unfamiliar neighborhood. There were several big grain silos on my left and a row of small houses on the right. I noticed one house with the lights still on. I ran to this house and banged on the door. The porch light came on and a very frightened woman poked her head out. I told her I needed to use the phone. She couldn't speak English! When I demonstrated calling someone, she reluctantly let me in and showed me the phone. I called Kay and Roger and told them what had happened. I didn't know where I was, and this woman couldn't help me out, so I told Roger about the grain silos. He knew where these were and shortly, I saw their car outside. I ran out and climbed into Roger's little VW bug.

On the way home, I told them all about my evening. When we got to their house, we called the police to report it and tell them about Dan. The train engineer had already called in earlier, and the police had found the vacated, wrecked car and had picked up Dan, who was still wandering aimlessly down the tracks. I learned later that Dan spent the night in jail. He came to visit me a few days later to apologize. I was very cool and told him how I had saved his life as well as my own. I also informed him how stupid it was to carry a loaded gun in the glove compartment, or anywhere else for that matter. I never saw him again, but I hope this experience knocked some sense into him.

Following this episode, I once again vowed that I would try harder to live more responsibly, concentrate more on my studies, not party every night, and not get drunk so often. Despite my determination, with the last vestiges of parental restrictions removed, my life remained out of control. I'm not proud of the lifestyle I lived in college, but viewing life on the scales of justice as I did, I had an inner struggle. On one hand, I knew I was losing this battle of the scales anyway so, I would rationalize, I might as well let it all hang out and do whatever I pleased, but then remorse would set in and I would strive to do better. But self-control eluded me and one night following a dare to drink an entire fifth of gin, I was so drunk I spent the whole night hugging the toilet throwing up thinking, *Dad's right, I am headed for the gutter.* My activities in the evenings, some I could remember, some I could not, would leave me guilt-ridden in the mornings. This destructive pattern of determining to improve, then failing completely, continued for months. I was miserable. Deep inside, there seemed to be a vacuum, an emptiness, a longing

I didn't know how to fill. I knew something was missing, I just didn't know what it was.

Paul, the writer of Romans, describes and comprehends this conflict much better than I did at eighteen when he writes about being a slave to sin, saying, "I know that nothing good lives in me, that is, in my sinful nature. For I have the desire to do what is good, but I cannot carry it out. For what I do is not the good I want to do; no, the evil I do not want to do—this I keep on doing" (Romans 7:18). Self-determination doesn't work. But I wasn't familiar with the writings of Paul and I'm sure I would have been offended if anyone had suggested I was a slave to sin, of all things.

My first Christmas vacation, I came home to find my bedroom was no longer my room. Everything I had left—my yearbooks, my clothes, my pictures, stuffed animals, etc.—all gone. Everything had been thrown out or given to Goodwill. As a vacuum is quickly filled, so had my space in this house. It was as if I had never existed. One of my presents was a trip to Aspen, Colorado to ski. I was to return the night before I was scheduled to go back to college. I got the feeling I wasn't wanted in Dallas. As you can imagine, this only added to my already growing despair, but I pushed aside the inner pain and set off to have a good time skiing.

Everyone has defining moments—moments that change the course of one's life. While in Colorado, I had one of those cathartic moments. I woke up with a man I had met the previous day. I got dressed and stumbled out. I had had enough. I wandered out to a snowy field, ashamed, numb, and very angry.

Why, I asked myself, *did you do that? How low are you going to sink?* I furiously started throwing snowballs at God, screaming, "You put us down here and expect us to be good, but there are all these temptations. Everywhere. How are we to be good? Are you just up there laughing at us because you've demanded something of us that we can't possibly do? How 'bout a little help, God?"

This wrestling match with God was a turning point in my life. God didn't speak to me that day, nor did things change; but this cry for help, this earnest plea to God, was heard. He was moving in a powerful way. I just didn't know it.

This is often true in our lives. We need help, we cry out to God, and because we see no immediate response, we think God is too busy, we think He didn't hear us, or He doesn't care. This leads us to think we have to take care of things ourselves. However, God is pleased when we ask for help. He hears an earnest plea. Often, that is all it takes for Him to move on our behalf. But once we ask, we need to wait on Him. We need to trust God even if we do not see any evidence of help.

With Christmas vacation over, I returned to Texas Tech. My roommate was a cute, sweet girl with one brown eye and one blue eye. One weekend she set me up with a blind date. The four of us went to dinner then to a movie. Her date was Jack Keels and my date was Steve Brownfield, but Jack and I immediately connected and spent the night flirting with each other, ignoring our own dates. I thought I had found what I was missing. I thought I had filled the void. Within a month, we eloped.

Jack grew up in Plainview, Texas, and his parents, Tallmadge and Charlotte, still lived there and ran a print shop. They had raised Jack in the Baptist church and he made a profession of faith at a very young age. They enjoyed telling me the story of the day the preacher said, "If anyone loves Satan, say Amen!" Seven year old Jack had been daydreaming and heard only the "say Amen," so he shouted, "Amen!" They liked me and thought that I would have a good effect on their son, settling him down, motivating him to study hard and do well. How funny! That's what I thought he would do for me. They agreed to help us financially while we were in school if we needed it. We got jobs, found a tiny duplex, and moved in our few belongings. Jack, along with enchanting dimples, curly long eyelashes, and a mischievous grin, had a very high IQ. This coupled with a great sense of humor and a love of debate made our life interesting, full, and fun.

Jack was a Christian. I thought I was a Christian. Soon we began having debates about whether I really was a Christian. He could drink just as much beer as I could. We both smoked. Church attendance was never considered. His life looked just like mine. What was the big deal? Just who did he think he was? Looking back, I don't know if he was inept at explaining the gospel or if I just wasn't listening. What I heard was that I was a sinner and he wasn't. I would carefully explain to him that in my life, I had stolen only one bottle of nail polish, which I'd taken back the following day due to remorse, I had never killed anyone, I never used the name of the Lord in vain, blah, blah, blah. I was defensive. What, I demanded, had he done that was so great? So magnanimous?

One evening we were invited to have dinner with Mark and Julie Duncan. Mark had been a good friend of Jack's when they were in high school and I had heard all about him. Mark thought that he might like to be a missionary and Mark's parents had asked Jack and his parents if Jack would accompany Mark to Peru for a short missionary trip. The purpose of this trip was to determine if this was really a good career choice for Mark. Jack's parents readily agreed, thinking this would be a good experience for him, and gave their permission. So, following their high school graduation, Jack and Mark flew to Peru, South America to begin a year of service.

Since both Jack and Mark's dads were printers, they had learned much about printing presses and they were to work in the print shop at Yarinacocha, the Wycliffe Bible Translator center in Peru. Kenny and Ginger Gammon were to keep an eye on them and assist them if they needed anything. I had heard all about this trip. Jack described it as a lark, a blast, a great adventure where they hunted for alligators, ate monkey eyes, and played pranks on all the other missionaries.

While there, Mark got very sick with Leishmaniasis, a form of leprosy causing fever, weakness, and skin irregularities. He struggled with this disease for eight of the twelve months they were in Peru and decided that foreign mission work wasn't for him. Jack, on the other hand, felt a strong call from God. He knew that this was what God wanted him to do with his life. Jack was an artist, however, and had long dreamed of becoming an architect. He didn't want to be a missionary. He told God that he would make a lot of money and support missionaries. If that wasn't good enough and if God still really wanted him to be a missionary, then God would have to give him a wife who wanted to be a missionary. When he met me, he breathed a sigh of relief, because he knew that I wasn't even a Christian. He called me a heathen. He was off the hook. And of course, he never let me in on this little deal he'd made with God. The dinner with Mark and Julie was dull. They were boring, lacked humor, and piously informed me *they* didn't partake of alcoholic beverages.

My marriage didn't have the anticipated effect on my studies. In fact, the opposite was true. I now focused my attention on learning how to cook and cleaning our little house, devoting even less time to studying. To my dismay, I failed out of school. I told myself I would go to summer school, take the required number of hours, make at least all Cs, and reenter in the fall semester on probation.

With that little problem solved, we took off for Colorado for a belated honeymoon. Before we reached the Texas state line, I began feeling nauseous. The following day, I woke feeling more exhausted than when I went to bed and still very nauseous, but we drove on to Colorado. *I better not be pregnant*, I thought, as we wanted to stay as a couple for a few years to get to know each other and have some fun before the responsibilities of parenthood fell to us. We had rented a small cabin tucked into the forest and Jack made some pudding for supper. I had no appetite, but since he had been so sweet to make it, I tried to force myself to eat some. The nausea soon turned to uncontrolled bouts of vomiting and by morning, I knew I was very ill.

We decided we had better head home; the lovely plans for hiking, exploring the mountains, and simply enjoying each other's company ruined. Our trip home took much longer because we had to pull over every thirty to forty minutes for me to open the car door and retch on the ground. We pulled into a gas station and while Jack filled the car, I went to the restroom. I washed my face and looked in the mirror. My eyes were yellow—even my skin looked yellow. Forget the disappointment over the honeymoon, now we were just very concerned about my health.

We ended up driving to Plainview instead of home, because it was Memorial Day weekend and Jack's family doctor had agreed to see me. Besides, it was closer than Lubbock. Dr. Johnson took one look at me and put me in the hospital in isolation. Diagnosis, infectious hepatitis, contracted four months ago in the dorm. Eighteen other girls had been or soon would be similarly diagnosed. I was in the hospital for three weeks, then sent home to rest in bed for three months and put on a no fat, high sugar diet. This is not the treatment of choice today, but in the late sixties, it was protocol.

We had ordered a trailer from my dad and this was delivered while I was in the hospital, so Jack alone drove to Lubbock to settle our new home into a nice little trailer park and move our things from the duplex. I was disappointed to miss all this; his parents couldn't even come see me while I was in isolation, but when I was finally released from the hospital, it was very nice to recuperate in our new home.

Day after day, I lay on the couch thinking about how I wasn't in school this summer, about how because of that, I wouldn't be going to school in the fall, about how I had wasted so much time. I thought of the many opportunities I had squandered, and about how, this time, I would reform. These three months with nothing to do but think were very good for me. I had matured to a degree and I knew it was time I acted accordingly. For the first time in my life, I wanted to be in school, but alas, I had failed out and wouldn't be allowed. I think this made me appreciate the opportunity when the following spring, Texas Tech did allow me to reenter on probationary status. When the ban was lifted, I did, at last, become a serious student.

I took eighteen hours, a heavy load, but I was trying to catch up and so, much of the spring, my nose was in a book. When we did find time to socialize it was usually with Kay and Roger, and while having dinner with them in their cute little house, Kay and I would talk about Michigan. We told the guys how beautiful it was, how beautiful Higgins Lake was, how blue and clear the water. It was a real lake, not a man-made lake, and when God makes a lake, it's far superior. During one of these dinners, we decided to drive to Michigan when the semester ended. So, that June, we all piled into Roger's VW and the four of us drove from Texas to Michigan. As teenagers, Kay and I often went to a dance hall, The Music Box, at Houghton Lake. We took the guys there and danced and laughed the wonderful night away.

After we returned to Texas, the four of us decided that Lubbock needed a teenage dance club like The Music Box. We rented a big warehouse, cleaned it up, slapped on some paint, and hired a band. The first few weekends The Music Box in Lubbock was opened were pretty sparse, but as word spread, we soon had hundreds of teenagers coming to hang out every weekend. We worked on the weekends and attended classes during the week, and by the end of summer, the money started rolling in and soon we all bought new cars. We were on top of the world, all was copasetic, and we enrolled in the fall semester with great optimism. *Finally*, I thought, *my life is under control.*

3

I DO BELIEVE

///

"For the word of God is living and active.
Sharper than any double-edged sword,
it penetrates even to dividing soul and spirit,
joints and marrow; it judges the thought
and attitudes of the heart."

HEBREWS 4:12

I came home from class one day to find a man sitting on the hood of his car in our driveway. He was reading his Bible. *Ugh, this is one of those Jesus freaks that Jack knew in Peru,* I thought. Sure enough, Kenny Gammon was in my driveway. Kenny was in town for a missions conference. I invited him in, and soon we were having a heated argument. He told me I was a sinner and needed a Savior. I told him I was a Christian—the same old argument I had had many times with Jack.

By the time Jack got home from class, Kenny and I had reached a stalemate. Kenny and Jack hugged the bear hug of long lost friends. Jack invited him to stay for dinner. I didn't want him to stay. After all, he had just called me a sinner. We argued. Jack won. Kenny would go to his host home, change clothes, and return for dinner on his way to the conference. While he was gone, I made a decision. I'm the intelligent one here, the open-minded one; I'll just show him how open-minded, intelligent people act. Not only will I fix and serve him dinner, I'll go to this mission's conference with him. So that night, Jack went to work at The Music Box and I accompanied Kenny to the missions conference.

This was my first missions conference and I didn't know what to expect. There were several speakers and all told exciting stories of their work on the mission field. At the end of the evening, the speaker, once again, stated that we were all sinners. Once again, I was offended. That night at home, I was fuming. I got out an old dusty Bible and plopped down on the couch. I was angry, offended, and very self-righteous. I was a woman with a purpose. I was going to find ammunition in the Bible and I was going to be armed and ready with these arguments for Kenny the following day. I opened the Word of God and flipped through the pages. I happened to turn to Acts 16. In this passage, Paul and Silas are in the middle of their second missionary journey. They had been arrested and were in prison. During the night, while they were singing, an earthquake shook the walls of the prison, opening the doors. The jailer woke up, terrified, as he knew if the prisoners escaped, he would have to pay with his life. He yelled, "What must I do to be saved?" Paul replied, "Believe in the Lord Jesus, and you will be saved—you and your household." I was stunned. *Is that all? Is that all? Just believe? Lord, I do believe.*

Just two years and three months after throwing snowballs and yelling at God, He tenderly reached down and spoke to me through His Word. A light turned on in my head. I understood. I finally understood. I had worked so hard trying to be good. But being a Christian has nothing to do with being good. It has nothing to do with good deeds. The scales of justice were my idea, not God's. What a relief. What an overwhelming sense of relief. I was very excited. I couldn't wait for Jack to come home to tell him. When he walked in, I announced that now I really was a Christian. We had our usual argument, but this time I had the right answers. This time I didn't spout off a list of all my good deeds. I showed him the place in the Bible where I had been reading. I showed him where it said you just had to believe in Jesus. He was soon convinced I was indeed a Christian.

The next day, Kenny came back to visit. Yesterday, this was a man I had disdained. In my ignorance and arrogance, I thought he was far beneath me, both in class and intelligence. But today, he was my brother! I flew out of the house. I hugged him. I loved him. I wanted to know everything he knew about God. I dragged him into the house and began firing questions at him. Needless to say, Kenny was amazed at this transformation from snobby pseudo-intellectual to hungry, eager learner, but soon he was rejoicing with me at my new birth and my newfound faith. That night, I couldn't wait to go back to the missions conference. Once again, Jack went to The Music Box and I went with Kenny.

This night proved to be another defining moment in my life—a turning point. Again the speakers talked of their experiences on the mission field. The last speaker told us there was a great need for many more people to go and spread the gospel, the good news of Jesus. He asked for a show of hands of people who would be willing to go if God called them. This wasn't a commitment—just, who would be willing? Most of the hands in the congregation went up. Mine wasn't among them. My first argument with God ensued. I knew God wanted me to go. I knew He was calling me. I also knew I didn't want to do this. How, you ask, did I know? I can't explain it other than to say, how did I know that I loved Jack? Did someone tell me? No, I just knew. That's how it was this night. I just knew. *Why are you asking me, God?* I thought. *Look at all these people who are willing— why not ask one of them?*

In high school, I had read *Through Gates of Splendor*. This is a wonderful story of faith and commitment. It is also a story of wild, violent Indians. *Are all Indians wild?* I wondered. *Does God really want me to go live among wild, violent Indians?* How little I knew of the mission field. The sum total of my knowledge added up to many misconceptions. These misconceptions were the basis of fear and uncertainty as I contemplated actually going to the mission field. I hope my experiences will eliminate for the reader any misconceptions of the mission field they have that might be holding them back from answering the call themselves. Truly, the harvest is plentiful and the workers few, and most Indians are in fact very friendly and mild.

Later that night, Jack came home and I announced, "I'm going to be a missionary, I hope you'll come." Without speaking a single word, he turned around and walked out the door. I sat down and began to pray. How wonderful to pray, knowing that your prayer is actually being heard, that someone who loves you, someone who is very powerful, is listening. I knew that somehow things would be put to rights. Two hours later, Jack came home and sat down beside me.

"I have something I need to tell you."

Out came the call in Peru, out came the promise to God, out came the confession of the relief Jack experienced when we married and I wasn't even a believer. We sat together holding hands. God Almighty had indeed called us. We knew this beyond all doubts. You can run, but you can't hide. We would follow this call. Thus began our journey. We would be missionaries.

4

THE TIME OF PREPARATION

"Study to show thyself approved unto God,
a workman that needeth not to be ashamed,
rightly dividing the word of truth."
2 TIMOTHY 2:15 KJV

We knew we wanted to do Bible translation. After my experience of finding the Lord, I knew that His Word was, indeed, the living Word. I wanted everyone to have this precious Word available to him or her. We mutually agreed that we wanted to join Wycliffe in their mission of putting the Word of God into the hands of every tribe. We also knew that we wanted to finish college. I was majoring in accounting and Jack architecture, neither very applicable to mission work. We did some research and decided we would move to Austin, transfer to the University of Texas, and study anthropology and linguistics. It took about a year to get this all in place. We sold our part of The Music Box to Kay and Roger and wound up our affairs as best we could.

In the sixties, we had the flower children, Woodstock, marijuana, and The Beatles. We were still innocent. That was about to change. Jack and I made plans to finish the summer semester at Texas Tech, and then move to Austin the last week of August, 1966. On August 1 of that year,

Charles Whitman terrorized the nation for ninety-six long minutes. He climbed the Tower at the University of Texas and from the observation deck, with a high-powered rifle, began shooting at students below. From his unassailable vantage point, he managed to kill fourteen people and wound dozens of others; some disabled for the rest of their lives. Later that day, the police found the bodies of Whitman's estranged wife and that of his mother. The plaza beneath the Tower was covered with blood; classes were suspended, our innocence gone forever. Needless to say, my excitement to move to Austin and attend the University of Texas dimmed.

This wouldn't be the only time I would be afraid to go where God led me. No, this was just the first of many times I would feel fear, but I was young and in love with my new Savior. I prayed and asked Him to give me courage. I had been a Christian a little more than a year now. After Kenny left Lubbock, I had bought a Bible and read it through three times that summer. I wasn't what you would call grounded in the Word, but I was much more familiar with it and I thought of the courage it took for Joshua and Caleb to cross the river and move into Canaan. Surely I could cross Texas and move to Austin. I prayed for the victims. I prayed for the family of Charles Whitman. I prayed for the students. Just twenty days after this horrible event, while Austin was still reeling, we moved our trailer to Austin and settled into a pretty little trailer park close to Barton Springs.

The next two years were filled with reading and studying. We took many classes together, which meant we could study together and pretty much have the same class, test, and exam schedule. During finals, we would study for several hours and then, about midnight, go play tennis for an hour so we could sleep.

Toward the end of 1967, I became pregnant with Kerry and for the next three months, I was tired, dizzy, and nauseated. My morning sickness lasted all day. Why, I wondered, did they call this morning sickness? Finally, I started feeling better and managed to take twelve hours in the spring semester. We had a morning final on June 5. Being very pregnant, plus being left-handed and sitting in a right-handed desk, I could hardly reach my paper. The exam consisted of one question, the answer of which I didn't know. I scribbled some nonsense, squirmed, and tried to get comfortable. I finally gave up and went home. For the rest of the day, I sat glued in front of the TV. Senator Robert Kennedy had been shot shortly after midnight. As he teetered between life and death, I began having contractions. I knew that I would be a mother very soon, but I didn't want a child born on the same day a Kennedy was shot. This was not to be. Kerry Ruth Keels was born just as Bobby Kennedy died. I failed the final.

The sixties marked a period of unrest. Betty Freidan and Gloria Steinem made the feminist movement very popular. Ralph Nader wrote *Unsafe at Any Speed*, causing Congress to require seat belts in all new cars. Rachel Carson wrote *The Silent Spring*, prompting Congress to ban DDT, so mosquitoes made a great comeback. Universities were in the early years of full integration. In July 1969, Neil Armstrong and Buzz Aldrin walked on the moon, and I graduated.

Lorrie was born that September and we moved to Dallas the next month. In January, we began a year's study at Dallas Bible College. Wycliffe Bible Translators is a faith-based mission, so during this time, we began raising support. We joined a Presbyterian church and worked in the youth department. Many of the friends we cultivated during this time supported our work for twenty years. What a blessing!

At that time, four months of training in the dark jungles of Mexico was the requirement of WBT. We decided to drive to "Jungle Camp," and the main office put us in contact with another family that wanted a ride. On January 14, 1971, Norm and Ivy Tattersoll, along with their baby Tracy, joined us on the long drive to Chiapas, located in the southern tip of Mexico. Kerry ate only Tang and oatmeal, Lorrie was still nursing, and both were in diapers. We left three days before the Dallas Cowboys played the Baltimore Colts in Super Bowl V. I was and continue to be an avid football fan; it would be five months before I knew that the Cowboys had lost 16-13 in the last five seconds of the game.

The four months we spent in the jungles of Chiapas, Mexico for our training were not only profitable, but a lot of fun. We met some wonderful people who remain friends today, learned lots of great stuff, and felt confident we were prepared to face whatever came our way. It had also been a welcome break from all the studying of the past years. I had learned to study, but wouldn't have considered it one of my favorite pastimes. All this considered, we were still thrilled to be heading home and on to the next step in our journey.

5

WE MEET THE GUAYABEROS

*"And how can they believe in the one
of whom they have not heard?
And how can they hear without
someone preaching to them?"*

ROMANS 10:14

We were excited to get to the field, and as soon as we returned home from Jungle Camp, we began the preparations. Visas, passports, shots and inoculations, and decisions—what to take, what not to take—all became part of our daily routine. We bought four 55-gallon drums and packed them to ship to Colombia via JAARS, Wycliffe's Jungle Aviation and Radio Service. They fly and maintain the planes, operate and maintain the radios, and ship things all over the world for the missionaries.

We gave stuff to friends and took loads and loads to Goodwill. Where did all this paraphernalia come from? How had we managed to accumulate so much stuff? Our church had a commissioning service and a reception for us. My folks, Kay and Roger, and their kids, Jimmy and Amy, all came to Love Field to see us off. There were tears, hugs, and kisses—and Mom gave us several Snickers candy bars to eat on the plane.

Finally, the moment arrived. The culmination of weeks and weeks of extensive preparations were over and we boarded the plane.

How ironic and what a blessing that Kenny and Ginger Gammon were working at the WBT office in Miami. I kidded Kenny, "Look what you got me into!" We spent a day with them before heading off to Colombia. It was July and their house was 80-plus degrees. No air conditioning—getting us prepared for the jungle, I guess. I don't think I slept an hour. At 3:00 a.m., we all got up to go to the airport to board the plane. We were supposed to leave at 5:00 a.m. The plane was three hours late, but we finally got off the ground. To save money, we had chosen Aero Condor. What a big mistake. What a horrible flight. We were forced to land in Barranquilla, Colombia because of a problem with one of the engines. We sat in that airport for seven hours until they finally decided that the engine was fixed. As we were taxiing down the runway, I could see the propeller out my window. It alternately stopped and started. I asked God to protect us in our foolishness, and vowed next time we would fly another airline, if there were a next time. There was.

It's not hard to describe what it's like flying off to parts unknown with two small children. In one word—terrifying! But, sweeter than Snickers is the Word of God. Some of my favorite verses that got me through many nights of wild, useless terror were Proverbs 3:5 and 6. A man in our church had given Jack a toolbox with these verses etched on the inside lid. How precious those verses have been to me. "Trust in the Lord with all your heart and lean not on your own understanding; in all your ways acknowledge him, and he will direct your path." Once again I thought of the courage of Caleb and Joshua crossing the river to Canaan, facing the giants with God exhorting them, "Be strong and courageous. Do not be terrified; do not be discouraged, for the Lord your God will be with you wherever you go" (Joshua 1:9). I reread the words on a card my grandmother had sent me, "How beautiful on the mountains are the feet of those who bring good news" (Isaiah 52:7). As I filled my mind with God's precious Word, my anxiety dissipated and I grew excited as

I contemplated bringing good news to people who walked in darkness, knowing God would be with me each step of the way.

We finally landed safely in Bogotá, Colombia. We spent two nights at the Group House, resting and meeting the staff there. Then we headed to Lomalinda. Lomalinda is the Wycliffe center and is located in the *llanos*, the plains of Colombia. South America is a beautiful continent. The Andes Mountains cut vertically through the middle and provide breathtaking scenery—and treacherous roads. Due to the altitude of these mountains, the small JAARS planes didn't often cross them. Lomalinda was about thirty miles southeast of Villavicencio, where a JAARS plane would pick you up and transport you to the center. The short forty-mile trip from Bogotá to Villavicencio traveling by bus or taxi over the Andes Mountains usually took four to five hours and was very dangerous. There were often mudslides, causing hours of delay, and many fatal accidents. Numerous white crosses line the narrow roadway testifying to the perils of this journey. Our trip to Villavicencio was uneventful and four and a half hours after leaving Bogotá, we pulled into the tiny airport at Villavicencio just as the JAARS plane was landing.

Unlike the tedious trip over the mountains from Bogotá to Villavicencio, the flight from Villavicencio to Lomalinda was less than thirty minutes, taking us over the beautiful *llanos*. How excited I was to see Lomalinda for the first time. From the air, I could see small houses perched on hilltops, the airstrip, and a lake. Lomalinda means pretty hills, and there were lots of hills and indeed it was very pretty.

Lomalinda served as Wycliffe's center of operations for all of Colombia. There was a hangar, commissary, post office, finance office, guest house, children's home, a school from kindergarten through high school, and a dining hall that also served as the church on Sundays. This is where the support personnel lived permanently. Support personnel included the pilots, radio and technical staff, teachers, children's home parents, and all the others it took to run this base of operations. The translators, like ourselves, built homes at Lomalinda and also in their tribal locations. Since we had no house as yet, we moved into the guest house, all four of us living in one room, wall to wall beds. Down the hall were two bathrooms centrally located, which we shared with five other families. As we had no kitchen, we ate in the dining room, which afforded us the opportunity to quickly get acquainted with the other missionaries.

The first year in Colombia was filled with orientation, language learning, starting construction on our house at Lomalinda, and deciding which tribal group to work with. By this time, I was pregnant again, so we wanted to get started building our Lomalinda house. Jack, having studied architecture for years in college, saw building our house as a great challenge. How did you design a 1400 square foot house, the limit set by the Wycliffe Colombian branch governing board, for a growing family, maintain good air flow for cooling a house in the tropics, and make it aesthetically pleasing, all at the same time? He succeeded on all accounts and when it was finally completed two-and-a -half years later, I loved our small, split level house at the center.

You may be wondering why it took so long to build such a small house. There were several reasons. First, there was a wait list and it was first come, first served. There were thirteen projects on the list when we first got to Colombia. Actual construction on our house didn't even begin for almost eighteen months after the time we submitted our plans. The construction crew could only handle a few projects at a time. The construction crew consisted of short-term volunteers from churches in the States and a few of the locals. The language barrier between the locals and the volunteers often meant doing things over, as instructions were frequently misunderstood. Supplies were often on order for months and arrived in the wrong order when they did finally get to the center. For example, there might be plenty of lumber, but no cement for the foundation. Finally, it did seem to be true that no one was in a hurry in South America—there was always tomorrow. Erv Miller, a young Mennonite, was serving in Colombia for two years and headed up the construction crew. Jack gave him the plans for our house with lots of explanations, and Erv assured us he understood what was wanted.

Construction of our house taken care of, we then turned our attention to tribes. The determination of just which tribe translators worked with was a joint decision between the administration and the translators. There were tribes that had been surveyed and were ready for translators, tribes where work had begun, but for one reason or another, the translators were no longer working there, and tribes that had yet to be surveyed.

John and Sjaan Waller had worked with the Guayaberos for several years. They learned the language and had begun translating. Unfortunately, most of their knowledge was in their heads. For health and various other reasons, they had been reassigned and were heading up a new venture. We were asked to take up the Guayabero work. Jack and I spent hours in prayer, thought, and discussion over this big decision. Finally, we decided that yes, this was where God would have us work. Now, all our attention was directed to our first tribal visit.

The Guayaberos lived in about eight small villages up and down the Guaviare River. The Wallers had built a small house in the village of Macuare, so we would locate in that village as well and use their old house. I'll never forget our first day in Macuare. As the plane flew out over the *llanos* en route to Macuare, my stomach was having its own private air show. Butterflies were bouncing. I rarely got sick in the air, even in turbulence, but today, my stomach was uneasy. We came to the end of the *llanos* and flew over the jungle. The *llanos*, the plains, are grasslands. The jungle is lush, dark green, and from above, looks like a thick carpet. This God-made carpet stretches for miles and miles in all directions.

Our pilot, Tom Smoak, had been to Macuare many times. For Jack, Kerry, Lorrie, and me (now four months pregnant), this would be our first time. I was very excited to meet these people we would work with for many years—the people I believed God had called me to, the people with whom we would share God's love and Word. Our people....

We circled the runway twice. I learned later this was to warn the people to get off the airstrip. All kids, dogs, and belongings—clear the way, we're coming in. Seeing a plane, even a small one, was a sight the

Indians never tired of seeing, and they ran in from their fields, the river, and out of their houses just to watch the plane land. I watched out the window as we circled and saw children waving frantically, jumping up and down, pointing and laughing. We landed, taxied back to the middle of the strip, and cut the engines. As if on cue, more than one hundred people rushed in at us. We got out of the plane and were in a sea of dark, small people, dark brown eyes all fixed on us, and we stared back at them. They rubbed my arms and stroked my hair. Kerry, four years old, had blond hair that hung to her waist. They stroked it, pulled it, and played with it. Next, they turned to Lorrie, now just three. She had strawberry blond hair and lots of freckles, a novelty to the people. In their fascination with the freckles, they poked and laughed at them. Wild Indians? Not hardly. I laughed to myself as I recalled thinking they might be wild and violent.

Tom was unloading our stuff and Jack was helping. The Indians grabbed the stuff and ran off with it. I wanted to tell them to come back with the stuff; we needed that stuff—it was ours! But who could have heard me in all the commotion and who could have understood me?

Everything I packed was the result of hours of planning and preparation. I had devised a list of items to take to the tribe. I hoped that this list of essentials would last during our first tribal visit. Among those essentials were salt, pepper, mustard, tomato paste, tomato sauce, flour, sugar, crackers, cocoa, peanut butter, graham crackers, raisins, beans, rice, tuna, pastas, baking soda, baking powder, powdered milk, coffee, canned vegetables, Kleenex, toothpaste, bath soap, laundry soap, and toilet paper. I hoped to be able to purchase meat and fish from the Indians, as well as some bananas, pineapple, and papaya during certain seasons, although I wasn't sure which seasons. With each trip back and forth between the center and the village, I revised this list by counting how many pounds, cans, jars of peanut butter, and boxes of these various items were left over. My system became very efficient.

I soon realized that I not only needed to revise what I packed, but how I packed. This first time, I made the innocent mistake of using boxes that I got in Puerto Lleras, a small town close to Lomalinda. The problem was that they happened to be liquor boxes and the Indians were well aware of this. Tearing open the boxes, hoping to find free alcohol, they were surprised to find a never-ending supply of dry goods instead. They proceeded to throw the food all over the place, laughing at the humor in this.

I had also packed a whole case of toilet paper that was wrapped in a large, clear plastic bag. Back in Texas, no one would have looked twice at this package. However, when the Indians saw this, we became the town's gossip for weeks to come. When one can afford a whole case of toilet paper, not just a single roll, in a village where people use leaves, they are considered wealthy. From that point on, I made it a point to divide up the rolls of toilet paper throughout the many boxes we packed, boxes that had not packaged liquor.

We followed the people down the trail to our new home—the home the Wallers had built. It was a structure about 20x50 feet, lifted five feet off the ground on stilts. We entered the house by climbing one of two ladders made of large, notched logs, located at the front and the back of the house. Half of the house was a large porch, where we hung four or five hammocks. The people gathered here. At one side, we had a little medicine room and a short wave radio. We strung a wire for the antennae out to some trees and we were to contact the center twice a week at a specified time. At other times, we called as needed.

At the back of the house was our kitchen, with a table and two benches on either side that were made out of raw planks. There was a short countertop, with shelves above and below, and a table where I put my Coleman stove. The kitchen's bark walls came up to just below waist high. It was open all the way up to the grass roof. Open and exposed. Very different than my North American kitchen, but quite pleasant. In the middle of the house, there was a room with full walls. This was the bedroom. There were two bunks as well as a wooden frame for a double bed, but instead of a mattress resting on those frames, there was a two-inch thick piece of foam. I had brought sheets and mosquito nets. We didn't have an outhouse, but Jack built one within a few weeks.

I was a bit discombobulated. To begin with, it was very hot, we were all thirsty, and there was no water. The stream was a half of a mile down the trail, and I would have to unpack our pots and pans and boil that water for twenty minutes, and then let it cool before we could drink it. I needed to make the beds and figure out how to hang the mosquito netting, but to complicate things, I had forty-five visitors on my porch all talking to me in a language I didn't understand. Everything we packed had been pulled out of the boxes and passed around for all to look at and comment on—but at least the unpacking was done, I mused. I would sort it all out later—in the dark I guessed, because I wasn't sure where the candles and matches were. Then, to my dismay, Lorrie had to go potty. I wasn't sure just where she was going to do this. I knew she would have an audience unless she went into the jungle and at three years old, no way was I sending her off alone.

We worked our way across the big porch, the bamboo strips of the floor bouncing and creaking with each step, sagging under the weight of so many people, as we made our way into the jungle. *Oh Lord, do wild beasts live in here? Are there tigers? Snakes? Please protect us.* Adding to my consternation, I then heard the plane take off. *Oh my, we have been deserted, left. Oh Lord, if I ever needed you, it's now!* At that moment, an idea popped into my head. Sing a song. So I started singing "Jesus Loves Me" and Lorrie joined me. Immediately, I felt better. I felt the presence of God and my panic began to subside. This idea of singing when fear creeps in has brought peace and comfort to this humble servant many, many times. God is faithful. I proudly thought my singing also probably served to scare off any wild thing that might have harmed us!

The Wallers had two 55-gallon drums (barrels). We rolled those out from under the house and found our pots; a couple of young girls ran to the stream, or *canyo* as it was called, and for a couple of pesos, they would bring back a big pot of water. They made several trips. We washed the barrels and positioned them at the corners of the house to catch rainwater. That day, we just filled them with what the girls brought.

Most of that first day, I sat on the porch and played with babies, smiled, and repeated words, much to the delight of the Indian women. I told them my name, Carolina, which they immediately changed to Carmelina.

Our new home was very near and just south of the equator. We were to learn that the sun rises and sets almost the same time year around. Also, if you're lucky enough to have a bathtub—which we didn't—the water actually drains and swirls in the opposite direction as it does in the US. We also learned that at dusk, mosquitoes came out in swarms and the Indians went home. We scurried around to find insect repellant, candles, flashlights, etc. as they left. We managed to find the Coleman stove, the bottle of gas, hook it all up, and boil some water. Our first meal in the tribe was oatmeal, powdered milk, and some bananas we had bought from the Indians. All this we ate by candlelight on our crude little table of planks and rough benches. Then we bathed with wet washcloths and started searching for sheets and mosquito netting. By the time the beds were made, nets hung, and prayers said, we all fell gratefully into our beds, thinking the first day in Macuare had come to an end. Little did we know.

The Wallers had told us to put a sheet of plastic on top of our mosquito net. I didn't know why, but did it nonetheless. A couple of hours later, I was awakened by the sound of rain pelting the plastic. Drip. Drip. Was the roof leaking? What was that squeaking noise? Drip. I reached for my flashlight and poked my head out of the plastic-covered mosquito net, shining the light up towards the grass roof, and there above us were hundreds of bats! While I was frozen with fear, staring up at them, one of them urinated on my face. Ugh! I squealed with disgust and quickly ducked back under the plastic. That wasn't rain I had heard.

I started to cry. This was going to be even harder than I anticipated. This was no picnic. Women often tell me that they could not have done what I did. The truth is, I couldn't either. I desperately needed God's help. I wanted to be as Paul, to be content whatever the circumstances— I wanted to believe I could do everything through Him who gives me strength. My life is not my own, I have been bought with a price, a tremendous price. It is not I who live, but Christ in me. The Word of God is powerful. Through all the years in Colombia, His precious Word enabled me to live in triumph. I was grateful for the many passages I had memorized. These passages came to my aid to battle self-pity, self-doubt, fear, and all my other weaknesses. Without these verses, I wouldn't have lasted two weeks at Macuare. That first night, however, with bats urinating over my head, I didn't look to the next two weeks, or even the next two days. I didn't dare. Instead, keeping my eyes firmly fixed on Jesus, blocking out the squeaking and the dripping, I managed to fall asleep. Maybe now the first day in Macuare had come to an end.

We awoke to the sounds of howler monkeys, the crying of hungry babies, women stirring up fires, Felipe's belching and singing, and women chopping wood to start their fires. The sounds and smells of a village waking up are unique and pleasant. When I smell a campfire today, my mind goes back to mornings at Macuare. The people were stirring—our people. Today I would visit them.

The second meal in the tribe was oatmeal. Oatmeal. Powdered milk. Bananas. This was our breakfast. Our few belongings were soon put up, and food was stored under beds. The organization made me feel better. I put a green and white-checkered oilcloth on our table. I poured boiling water over coffee grounds in a plastic cone lined with a filter, sat down, and had my first cup of coffee in Macuare. It was really quite nice. Home sweet home.

After breakfast, the girls and I went to the village. Jack was working with some of the men. We had decided in the night that we needed to build a little shelter for an outhouse and another little shelter to take tub baths. The galvanized tub we brought and two buckets of water made a nice sit bath for the girls. I took a pitcher and poured water over myself while standing in the tub. Not the shower shown in *House Beautiful*, but it achieved the goal of cleanliness, nevertheless.

Our tribe was a small tribe. There were about eight hundred Guayaberos living in six or seven small villages up and down the Guaviare River. Macuare was one of these villages. There were about eight families numbering about one hundred people. There were three houses on our side of the airstrip and five on the other side. The trail to the *canyo* (stream), a half-mile away, went right past our house. There was a trail leading to the river about a mile and a half away on the other side of the airstrip.

Most of the houses in Macuare looked like ours, only smaller. They were built up on stilts, had split bamboo for floors and walls, thatched roofs, and notched logs. Their roofs extended over an area of just dirt. This is where they had their fires. The women made big round clay cooking skillets. These were three to four feet in diameter, black, and had a lip around them. These were used to cook *cassava*, which the women were cooking this morning.

Cassava bread is the main staple food in the tribe and is made from bitter yucca plants. Bitter yucca grows in the ground like a turnip or a carrot. Mothers and young women, as young as eight years old, would go out in the early morning hours to dig up the yucca and wrap it in bundles, each weighing between fifty to one hundred pounds in total. They would come back in the late afternoon with this heavy load of yucca cascading down their backs, strapped to their foreheads, babies hanging in a sling in the front, smaller children lagging behind. Cassava contains dangerous amounts of a poison called hydrocyanic acid. Extracting these juices is a long process. When cooked, it forms flat bread, much like pita bread, and can measure up to four feet in diameter. The Indians would break it up into pieces and store it in cloth bags, to be eaten with soup, stew, or beans later on. Fresh cassava is quite tasty, but beyond that first day, the cassava bread turns dry and bitter, and tastes quite like a piece of cardboard.

That first morning, we watched them make cassava. The novelty of the freckles, strawberry blonde hair and light skin had worn off, and while they always loved Kerry's long blonde hair and brushed it often, they weren't touching it continually. The children wanted the girls to play, and of course my girls were only too happy about this; soon they were off running with the gang.

Guayabero children are beautiful. Their dark eyes, fat cheeks, and black shiny hair are stunning. I never grew tired of looking at them, watching them, and talking to them. The little girls wore handmade dresses and were taught to be modest. The little boys wore nothing until about eight or nine. The little boys all had bows and arrows that they made themselves, and they could actually shoot grasshoppers, small snakes, and mice. Boys had very little responsibility until they married at age thirteen to fifteen years, but their play with these bows and arrows taught them to be good hunters. At about ten years of age, they were given real bows and arrows and accompanied the men on hunts. Little boys also played with machetes. Initially this horrified me, but to my surprise, I never treated a cut that was the result of the little boys playing with machetes.

Little girls, however, had tremendous responsibilities. If Mama had a baby, the older sister helped care for the baby even if she herself were only four years old. Mom would take all the kids to the fields—little boys would shoot their arrows, little girls tended babies, and older girls would help dig and plant or dig and harvest the yucca. It wasn't uncommon for a small girl to walk into the village bent over with fifty pounds of yucca strapped on her forehead hanging down her back. These young girls also helped in preparation of cassava and gathering firewood, tending fires, and cooking fish and meat.

We soon learned the village had three chiefs—Moises, Felipe, and Alberto. We never did figure out why three chiefs, but it seemed to work. Moises' wife was Mer. They had six daughters. Their house was in disrepair. Moises often complained that if he had sons to help build his house it would be better. As it was, the roof leaked badly, the floor was gone, and they lived on the dirt.

Felipe, his younger brother, saw himself as the real chief. Moises was often drunk on the sugar cane brew, *guarape*, that the Indians made, so Felipe assumed the head chief role during these drunken bouts. He knew a couple of hymns the Wallers had taught them, and he sang one very loudly every morning for the whole village to see how spiritual he was.

Then he belched and we all knew it was time to get up, usually about 5:30 a.m. We never needed an alarm clock in Macuare.

Alberto lived across the airstrip and was very reserved, serious, and industrious. He spoke good Spanish and could do simple mathematics, so he was consulted by the people for buying and selling, acting as liaison to neighboring Colombians. Alberto was the only Indian we met that actually got rid of his first wife, casting her out and claiming a younger one. The first wife soon died with no husband providing meat or shelter for her. The new wife was about the same age as Alberto's oldest son, Pablo. The whole family was shamed by this act and was never again fully accepted by the tribe. This is a shame culture, behavior being enforced by shame. There are no police, courts, or lawyers to enforce laws, just the taboos passed down from generation to generation to shame if you didn't abide by them.

Our days passed quickly and soon we fell into a routine of treating cuts and parasites, visiting the people in the village, watching, observing, and listening. We were unable to hire a language helper, as the Indians were suspicious. For years they had trusted the Wallers, and they had left. Then we came. They had a great fear we were going to learn their language, then sell it—exploit them, or take it away from them somehow. We learned this much later. They would point to stuff and say, "Aat tsa is'm?" We decided this meant what's the name of that? So we started saying, "Aat tsa is'm" to them and they would say words. We pointed at things and wrote down phonetically what they said. For instance, we would point at a tree and say, "Aat tsa is'm," then write down the word they gave. Next day, the word had changed and we soon learned that they were mixing up the words. They might give us the word for "arm" as "boat" one day, and then the next person would give us the word for "leg" when we pointed at the arm. It was all very frustrating and confusing. We managed to study the phonology, but not the morphology or syntax.

One day some little girls were on my porch with their baby brother and I took him, cooing to him as mothers do; I said to the girls, "Aat tsa is'm?"

They giggled and said, "Whoo'hil."

I proceeded to bounce him on my knee saying, "Whoo'hil, whoo'hil," thinking this was his name. The little girls laughed and laughed. At dinner, I commented on his name, Whoo'hil, and wrote it down. Months later we learned that *whoo* means, "name" and *hil* means, "there isn't any." So what the little girls had said was he doesn't have a name, there isn't any name. No wonder they laughed as I bounced him on my knee cooing, "Hey little no name, little no name."

We also found out later that small children are not given names. When they are seven or eight, they choose their own names. They are given names at birth that are Spanish names only, because the neighboring Colombians all have names and made fun of the Indian children who had no names, but these were not their tribal names, and often the parents would forget this name.

The people met each Sunday. This they called a church service. The women sat on one side, the men on the other. They sang a few hymns the Wallers had taught them. The women sang much faster than the men and always finished first, looking very proud. Felipe was usually the "pastor," but Alberto or Moises could also assume this role. This time was used to vent frustrations and chastise the people for their laziness. These meetings were more like a town meeting. We attended these meetings while we were at Macuare, observing their culture, getting our ears accustomed to their language.

We completed the outhouse and a bathhouse. We hung wire clothesline and rigged up two tubs for washing clothes. We had begun establishing a positive relationship with the people. Jack and I both treated their cuts, parasites, and TB. Parasites included roundworms, whipworms, tapeworms, and amoeba. At least ten people had TB. We also passed out vitamins. One mother brought her little girl to me, and as she looked malnourished, I treated her for worms and also gave Mom a small bottle of vitamins and told her to give her daughter one a day, communicating in Spanish and many hand gestures, sun rising and setting, sleeping, etc. The next day, she was back for more vitamins. Evidently my gestures had not been successful. That afternoon, her husband came. He spoke a little Spanish.

"Did your wife give your daughter the whole bottle of vitamins?"

"Yes."

"Did she not understand that she was to give her just one a day?"

"Yes."

"Then why did she give her the whole bottle?"

"If one is good, twenty must be a lot better."

That was the first and last time we dispensed more than a day's dose of drugs. If they were on antibiotics, we just told them to come back the next day and we kept records of who was on what medication. The children loved the chewable vitamins and soon each day many were coming to the porch, yelling, "Vitamina, Carmelina; vitamina, Carmelina."

We spent four and a half months with the Guayaberos and felt this first time had been productive, but I was now eight months pregnant and needed to return to Lomalinda. The Guayabero midwives had offered to help deliver my baby, but I said, "Thanks, but no thanks." We knew they didn't trust us and that they still lied to us about the language. However, many people kept asking us if we were coming back and when. As we stood around the plane saying good-bye, we assured them, yes, we would return. The whole village was there to see us off and as the plane lifted off and circled, my heart was full of praise to God, for with His help, I had conquered fear of the great unknown, bats urinating on my head, six-inch-long cockroaches, and yes, even wild Indians.

6

A WILD PIG

///

"And there before me was a great multitude
that no one could count, from every nation,
tribe, people and language, standing before
the throne and in front of the Lamb."

REVELATION 7:9

We flew back to Lomalinda and I awaited the birth of our third child. Since Lomalinda had been an operating branch for almost thirty years, there were plenty of houses, and the common practice was, if a house was empty due to owners being on furlough or in the tribe, someone could stay there. The convenience was great. Not only were the houses furnished, they came complete with pots, pans, and linens. If all the houses were occupied, as usually happened at the annual conference, you could move into the guest house, which had the six rooms and two bathrooms.

On this occasion, the Hopis were on furlough and we moved into their house. My sister Mary came to spend the summer with us and worked part time in the finance office. Joy was born later than expected and Mary left for the United States just seven hours after her birth. Little did I know how much I would need her. I developed a uterine infection, had a fever of over 105 degrees, and was delirious for several days. Our neighbor, Jan Whistler, had a baby herself, and was therefore able to nurse Joy for two of these days. Everyone on the base brought ice, and they took turns rubbing my arms and legs with icy cold dishtowels. Jack was very concerned, and on the second evening, leaned over me and with a cool wet washcloth, wiped my feverish forehead. I looked him in the eye and clearly stated, "I'm going to see Jesus and I'm excited, but I don't know why He is giving you three little girls to raise alone."

Of course I was delirious and didn't recall this conversation when the fever eventually left me. The next night, Dr. Altig parked himself by the bed and didn't leave my side for more than a few moments at a time all night long. How blessed we were to have such qualified, godly physicians caring for us. This was truly the body of Christ in action. Thanks to God, antibiotics, and Dr. Altig, I made a full recovery.

The Hopis returned from furlough, so when Joy was only ten days old, we moved again, this time to the Headland's house. They were in the tribe and we could have their house for a month. Jack did all the moving, as I was still very weak and had my hands full caring for a baby plus two toddlers. I soon regained my strength, however, and we were anxious to return to the tribe, so when Joy was only a few months old, we flew back to Macuare. Grandma Charlotte, eager to share in our tribal experience, had come to Colombia and went with us. Joy had red hair and the Indians loved her. They called her *soi*, which in their language means "red." Grandma Charlotte they called *koaema* because it rhymed with grandma. This means, "chicken" and, of course, another excuse to laugh. They laughed so often at this that we finally had to tell Charlotte what it meant. As you can imagine, she wasn't very happy at being called a chicken. The two months *koaema* spent with us were great. To have the help was neat, but the fellowship of another woman, a believer, was wonderful, and I realized just how lonesome I got in the village. While she was visiting, Felipe's wife had another baby. They named her Carlotta, the Spanish equivalent of Charlotte, and of course Charlotte was thrilled.

The language learning continued to be a challenge. When a plane was coming, we would talk by radio and communicate with the pilots and let them know the weather report and how much cloud cover we had. The people were always excited to see the plane. They would gather on the porch—there were always numerous Indians on the porch while we were giving this weather report. So, when Charlotte's plane was scheduled to come, Jack walked outside and was looking up at the clouds to see what kind of cloud cover we had.

"There aren't any clouds, are there?" one of the Indians called out.

That's the standard question. If there's anything, or if there's not, the Guayaberos have a negative approach to this. Instead of asking, "Is there any?" they'll ask, "There isn't any?" They would come to the porch and say, "Medicine *i'hik.*" There isn't any medicine is there? And we would answer, "*Chae'ex.*" Yes, there is medicine. So Jack had gone out to look at the clouds and they asked this question and Jack said, "*Cha'ex,*" meaning, "Yes, there is," or so we thought. Everybody just started roaring. Seeing the Indians on the porch—it was as if he'd just told the biggest joke—all of them howling in laughter. When you're learning a language and you say something that makes everyone laugh, this gives you a big clue that something is wrong. We knew something was incorrect, we just didn't know what.

That evening we were sitting around talking about it and we went through all our notes. *Cha'ex* means, "Yes, there is." *What would "cha'ex" mean in relation to these clouds?* we asked ourselves. We broke down the word, analyzed and compared lists and lists of words from our notes, and finally came up with the answer. *Cha* was a prefix meaning "inside," and "*ex*" was a suffix meaning to sit. So, when Jack had gone out and they asked, "There isn't any clouds?" what he actually said in response was, "Yes, the clouds are sitting inside." I have to admit—we were pretty funny at times and had to laugh at ourselves.

Before going to the field, I'd asked a veteran missionary to give me some advice. Without hesitation, she said, "Do not allow bitterness to creep in and keep your sense of humor." Many times during the years that we worked with the Guayaberos, considering how they laughed at us all the time, we certainly needed to keep our sense of humor. We didn't always have success doing this. Macuare was lonely, dull, and boring. We often felt isolated. Being laughed at continually nibbled at our confidence. This, in fact, became the single most difficult aspect for me as I lived among the Guayaberos. We would discipline our girls. They would laugh. Were we doing the right thing? We tried to speak their language. They would laugh. I hung the clothes on the line. They would laugh. I boiled the dishes three times a day to kill germs. They laughed at that. Any newcomer to the village was brought back to the kitchen; "Look at that. That lady boils her dishes. See, she's really cooking them." And they'd laugh and laugh.

I would question myself—was it really necessary to boil my dishes three times a day? I became very aware of the importance of the support we receive from people who share our values. Affirmation, support, acceptance, encouragement, understanding— all culturally learned behaviors, were lacking here in this village where shame was the motivator. Behaviors I had never given much thought to now filled my thoughts. These important mores were missing, not just for us, but for the Indians as well. As hard as this was for me, I knew that it must not be much fun for the Indians either. I committed this matter to prayer and tried to keep my humor fully intact.

The next year passed quickly but our language acquisition was tediously slow. Our knowledge of this language grew bit by bit as we fought for each little piece of data. When we were positive of the meaning of a word, it was like a victory and we put it in a special book, the lexicon. Language learning under any circumstance is difficult and there were times when we wondered if we would ever be able to speak to the Guayaberos in their own language. Our frustration and discouragement mounted, and I asked, *Oh Lord, how long before you will send a language helper?* We pleaded our case before God Almighty.

Once again, we headed back to Lomalinda, this time for the birth of our fourth child. We moved into Hugh and Marty Tracy's house as they were on furlough. Construction on our house had begun and was near-ing completion. With us being at the center, things moved along faster, and in early December, we finally moved into our own home. In the two and a half years we had lived in Colombia, with all the coming and going to the tribe and back, we had moved over twenty times, each time into a different house on the base. Now, finally, we had permanent housing and unpacked the four 55-gallon drums that we had packed and shipped three years before. It was wonderful. The generosity of missionaries let-ting new families move into their houses was great, but now, we could actually put our clothes in closets and chest of drawers and leave them there.

When I describe our life on the mission field, one of the biggest confusions is always centered on our living arrangements. It was re-ally very simple. We had a tribe house. This house was in Macuare, had no indoor plumbing, no electricity, and no running water. We also had this new house in Lomalinda. This house did have indoor plumb-ing, electricity, and running water. I had a gas range and a refrigerator. Although this house was small for six people, with electricity and run-ning water, it always seemed like a palace to us when we returned from the tribe. When we lived at Macuare, I homeschooled the girls; when we lived at Lomalinda, they went to the school with all the other mis-sionary children.

The living arrangements even confused Lorrie once. We had just re-turned from the tribe and several women were in my living room bring-ing over casseroles, cookies, and fruit for our dinner. The girls were play-ing outside with friends and Lorrie rushed in and said she had to go potty. I told her that was great, go ahead and go. Ten minutes later, she came running back in and informed me she couldn't find it. Poor thing, she was looking outside for the outhouse, not remembering we had in-door plumbing.

Our girls loved living at Lomalinda. They were free to roam all over the base. They knew everyone and everyone knew them. They could ride their bikes to visit friends, go swimming at the lake, or go to the commissary when donuts came in and eat four or five donuts. At Lomalinda, when children turned thirteen, they could start driving a motorcycle.

The Lomalinda school wasn't far from our house, and the girls walked or rode their bikes to school if it wasn't raining. There was a shortcut they often took when they walked. They walked down the numerous steps we had carved out of our steep hill, then entered a small grove of palm trees and walked on logs over a small stream through the grove then onto a dirt road to the school. Kerry was skipping and singing as she made her way home one afternoon and as she walked across the logs, balancing over the stream, a movement caught her eye. She turned and found herself staring at an eighteen-foot long snake. Panic gripped her, causing her to almost lose her balance as she ran off the log into the clearing and up the many steps cut into the hill. She burst into the kitchen, white faced, out of breath, heart pounding and yelling about the snake, the huge snake.

We ran to get our neighbor Jesse, who just happened to be home, and he ran to the stream with Kerry, machete in tow. That was the biggest snake we saw while living in Colombia and I took pictures of it as several kids held it up, now dead and less fearsome.

At suppertime Kerry related in detail her very exciting experience. She said the first thing that popped into her head was, "In my Father's house are many mansions; if it were not so, I would have told you" (John 14:2).

"Why," I asked, perplexed. "Why, that particular verse?"

"I don't know, Mom. It was the only one that I could think of."

One fun thing worth mentioning was mud sliding. In rainy season, the torrential downpours caused streams and waterfalls in the hills and the kids would slide down these. The repeated sliding of many kids caused the surface to turn to mud. These slippery, muddy paths provided hours of fun for the kids at Lomalinda, leaving them covered in mud. I would hose down the girls before they came into the house for a shower. One afternoon, Lynn Hendrickson and I decided that we were missing out on too much fun, so we donned our old clothes and ran out the door to go mud sliding ourselves. It was fun, I have to admit.

But all this was yet to be, as we were just now unpacking and moving in our new home. We didn't have much to unpack, but it was such a comfort to see my own dishes, sheets, towels, and some different clothes. Some of the clothes we had brought for Kerry and Lorrie, they had long since outgrown, but that wasn't a problem, as we now had Joy and another child arriving any day.

Three weeks after we moved into our new home, Janey was born. This time there were no complications. Dr. Altig was home on furlough. An older doctor, Dr. Cunningham, was taking his place. He had delivered hundreds of babies in rural Alabama, and assured us he knew what he was doing. A friend of mine, a single lady, wanted to see a birth, so I had agreed to call her. Another young newly married gal wanted to see a birth before she actually tried to have one naturally, so I said she too could come. Of course, JoAnn Forester, the nurse, was there. So, I had three women, Jack, and Dr. Cunningham all in the bedroom with me. The problem was, the day before Janey arrived, Dr. Cunningham had wiped out on his motorcycle and had four broken ribs and was moving very slowly—too slowly. Despite having all these people to help, Janey and I managed her birth unaided. Dr. Cunningham said, "Oh, a little boy." Jack and I looked more closely. Had we missed something? "No, another precious little girl!"

Dr. Cunningham has since gone home to be with the Lord. He is fondly remembered.

The news from the United States wasn't good. For many years, we subscribed to *Time* magazine, which always arrived a month late. In 1972, as part of Richard Nixon's re-election effort, a massive campaign of political spying and dirty tricks was initiated against Democrats—Republicans planting bugs inside the offices of the Democratic National Committee. How did they think they could get away with this? They didn't. Two years later, our nation found itself in the midst of a criminal investigation unlike any other—the Watergate Scandal. Seeing that he would lose the impeachment vote, Richard Nixon resigned from the presidency of the United States on August 9, 1974. He remains the only president to resign this office. We didn't learn of this historic event for several months. I mention this only because it's hard to imagine life with no Internet, no cell phones, no Fox News. Today, current events are known almost immediately. This wasn't the case on the mission field of the sixties and the seventies. We relied on friends and family to write letters, old magazines, and the occasional reception of shortwave radio. It seems so strange now that we were so out of contact with the rest of the world.

In our little corner of the world, we continued working with the Guayaberos. Two more years passed and still no language help. We had lived with this tribe four years—four long years. We were discouraged. How, we asked ourselves, were we to teach the Guayaberos about God when we couldn't communicate? How would we ever translate the Scriptures in their language if they wouldn't teach us their language? We believed that the Guayaberos would be included in that great multitude that would one day stand before the throne. We still believed God wanted us there, so we figured surely He must have a plan. We just needed to wait on and trust Him.

The fruition of waiting the months and months that had long since turned into years ended one rainy Sunday afternoon, and I remember it like it was yesterday. Jack and I were swinging in hammocks on the porch and a young man, Vicente, came up to us.

"I am going to help you learn the language," he said.

"When do you want to start?" Jack asked him.

"Tomorrow."

"Good. I'll see you at first light."

Vicente walked away. We looked at each other. Not wanting to trust them after four long dry years, we didn't let ourselves get too excited. You can imagine our joy and delight when at 5:00 a.m. sharp, Vicente arrived and called out; he was ready to help. Thus began a partnership that lasted for many years.

Vicente was a good teacher. He and his wife didn't have children, but they knew how to talk to children, and Vicente decided to teach us as if we were children. He would tell little stories. We put these stories on tape loops and played them over and over again, memorizing them. The kids memorized them. These stories were humorous and had little relevance to real life, but taught us the language nonetheless.

> "*atit na lical*
> *atit na lical jan*
> *we fo tat*
> *we fo tat na lical*"

The kids would chant this to the Indians when they passed by our house on their way to the river. The Indians laughed. I prayed they were not saying something lewd or offensive. Later we learned what it meant.

> "A pig bit me,
> a wild pig bit me.
> When I went to my fields,
> he bit me."

No wonder the Indians laughed.

While we studied the language, our children adjusted well to tribal life. They never lacked for playmates or things to do. Running around the fields between our house and Jack's study, they found several bushes with clusters of black fruit. They brought some to me; I thought they must be wild blackberries and gave them a bucket to pick more. The Indians laughed and giggled as Kerry and Lorrie began filling the bucket. The Indians began eating the berries out of the bucket. Kerry and Lorrie began eating. For all this picking, they brought me very few berries. I made muffins with the berries, which they shared with the Indians. The Indians loved these muffins and thereafter encouraged this berry picking.

The *canyo* was a ten-minute walk from our house. Our house was in a clearing, but the path to the *canyo* quickly entered the jungle. The temperature dropped noticeably and was cool and breezy. The girls often removed their shoes while walking down the trail to feel the cool ground.

Sunlight shown through some leaves; other places were almost dark. When the shafts of sunlight hit you, it felt like magic.

Sugar cane grew along parts of the trail and the little boys chopped off stalks for the girls. I told the girls not to eat this stuff, as it would rot their teeth, but no child could resist chewing the stems, sucking the sweetness, and enjoying the feel of juice as it ran down their chins. The last part of the trail was a little hill. From the top of this hill, you could see the stream running through the trees. They slid down this last part, laughing, shouting, and enjoying childhood.

Butterflies. Around the stream were literally hundreds of bright, beautiful butterflies. They were all colors, but predominately bright yellow. This image still fills Lorrie's mind; "It's as if my child's mind knew I was seeing God and captured the image so perfectly and securely in my mind that I will never forget it."

After a dip, lying on the beach, cold and wet, the heat of the sun felt good. If you were still long enough, the butterflies would come drink the water droplets off your skin.

There was a "jump tree." The tree angled steeply out over the water. There were forks at about ten, twenty, and forty feet. Everyone could jump from the ten-foot fork. Each year, the girls would be a little braver and jump from a higher fork. The day came when they reached the forty-foot fork. Hesitation at the top caused shouting from below. Both English and Guayabero languages, phrases they didn't understand, yet communicating just the same—"Jump! Don't be a coward, hurry up! We want a turn."

And then, the jump, the panic right before hitting the water. Then silence as you plunged deeper and deeper into the cool dark water. The bottom was mushy, squishy, and soft. You shoved off, hoping your feet wouldn't stick. Breaking the surface, everyone would be laughing and talking at the same time, deciding who would climb next.

We had a lemon tree and several mango trees in our yard. The lemons grew big and juicy. Jack said it was because it was right by the outhouse, so it was constantly being fed and watered. The girls loved to climb the mango trees, grab a mango, bite into the skin, and pull off the peel. They would bite and spit, bite and spit, until all the skin was gone. The first few bites were the best. The stringy fruit would get stuck in their teeth as they got closer to the pit. Then, they craved salty foods, so off to the lemon tree. You didn't want to pick a juicy lemon. Juicy lemons were harder to eat. The kids played a game. They would pick lemons and decide for each other who would eat what lemon. Then everyone would tear the lemon assigned to them in half and begin eating it. The object was to eat the entire lemon without making a face. The Indians were much better at this game than my girls. After someone made a face, they salted the lemons and finished them off, sourness and all.

For several years we planted a garden. Many mornings, wild pigs would wander into our yard, rooting in the garden. Joy and Lorrie were the best at getting them to leave. Very early in the morning, they would run down the ladder, grab a stick, and run, screaming at the wild pigs in their long nightgowns and rain boots, beating on any pig that came too close. This also got them out of washing the breakfast dishes. Kerry preferred washing dishes to chasing pigs.

Wild pig. Wild pig—the first words Vicente had given to us many months ago. The first words we had been given in honesty. The first words we had written down in confidence. My heart warmed as I recalled those first few days of Vicente's help. It was always with a grateful heart that I watched Joy and Lorrie chase wild pigs from our yard.

7

A HARD LESSON

///

"To the weak I became weak, to win the weak.
I have become all things to all men so that
by all possible means I might save some."
1 CORINTHIANS 9:22

The dry season, January through March, was the best time to dig a well. You could dig deeper, as the water level was lower. We had dug a well in the village for the people. The water, being germ and parasite free, improved their health. Now, we wanted a well right outside our house. Rick, a young college student, came to help us dig the well. He would dig the well, while we continued language analysis.

By the time the first well was finished, most of the people had laughed themselves out at the crazy notion of our digging for water. There were two brothers from another village, however, who had not witnessed the first digging and happened to be visiting while Rick dug. One of the brothers laughed so hard, we began to call him "Laughin' Louie." I guess trying to get water from out of the ground would seem funny if you weren't educated about it. Well, Rick would put on a little coolie hat, crawl down in his hole, and whistle the theme song from *The Bridge Over the River Kwai* while the little boys threw pebbles in on his head. Laughin' Louie and his brother would come to laugh.

It was a long hot summer and we were all getting tired of the ridicule. All discussions with Laughin' Louie and his brother about Christ just brought on more laughter. I argued with God. "You know, if we're going to be good witnesses to these people, they've got to respect us. They've got to see that we're smart and that we actually have something to offer." I thought about this often—it filled my thoughts and my prayer life. I had the misconception that some successes would make us credible. Then Laughin' Louie might think, "These people *do* know what they're doing. They can dig a hole in the ground and come up with water. They're not the idiots we think they are. Maybe their message is worth looking at." And so, once again, I struggled with this issue. I thought it was important that we didn't look like fools all the time.

After we got the well going, the first month or so, we were hauling out lots of muddy water as the clay was still settling. We'd have hours during the day when we'd have nice, pure water, but as soon as Laughin' Louie would walk down the trail, it would turn cloudy and he would laugh and say, "See, I told you that well wouldn't be any good." Then he would move to the edge of the well and kick a little dirt back in on Rick. Rick, too, was getting pretty weary of this—the pebbles, the dirt, and the laughing. One day when he was standing outside the hole, Laughin' Louie came up and grabbed his elbow, and Rick turned around and punched him. We all felt bad and later Rick went to the village to apologize. The Guayaberos have no words for "I'm sorry" or "I apologize," so to do so presented a challenge. I'm not sure just what Rick said to Louie, but I saw them later laughing and talking together, so it must have been successful. I still wanted a little success so we wouldn't look so stupid in the eyes of the people.

A few months after we dug the well, Laughin' Louie's wife had a baby and she had trouble with the delivery. When women have trouble with the delivery, they usually bury the baby—they'll bury the baby if it's twins, if it's deformed, or if for any reason they don't want the baby. The moment of birth a decision is made—if they decide to keep the baby, they do, but if they choose not to, they bury the baby alive, facedown. Laughin' Louie's wife was having trouble with the delivery and she decided even before the birth that she would bury the baby. When we heard this, we told the people, "Please don't let her bury the baby. Bring it over here and we'll take care of the baby." As you would imagine, all day long every time someone came down the path, we looked up thinking we were going to have a little baby in the house pretty soon. We weren't sure what we'd do with it. On the third day, the woman herself came with the baby. She had jerked the cord loose in anticipation of burying the baby, but had miraculously changed her mind. There was nothing left on the navel—no cord to tie off. We had two books, *The Medical Manual* and *Donde No Hay Doctor*, that helped us tremendously. These books were as worn as our Bibles. We looked in *The Medical Manual* and it said that when you deliver a baby, be sure you don't pull the cord completely loose or the baby will die. Well now, that wasn't very helpful.

So here we were with this baby, now three days old, and she'd been bleeding for these three days. We couldn't get hold of Lomalinda because it was the noon hour. We didn't really know what to do. We took the baby to the kitchen, laid her down, and put a diaper on her stomach. Within thirty minutes, the whole diaper was saturated with blood. As I walked towards the bedroom, I heard Kerry and Lorrie praying for this little girl and I just knew that God would spare this baby—that He would hear the prayers of my little girls. After lunch, we were able to reach Dr. Cunningham on the radio. He instructed us to put Phisohex around the cord and apply direct pressure. To get the bleeding stopped, we had to apply a lot of direct pressure. My thumb pushed almost to the table, almost to the backbone of this baby. We could only do this for thirty minutes to an hour before our arms started to cramp, so Jack, Rick, and I took turns. Every time we let up it would start to drip. After seven hours of applying direct heavy pressure on the baby's stomach, the bleeding finally stopped. For most of these long hours, she had been too weak to even object. We made a big ball of adhesive tape, put it on her navel, and then wrapped more tape around her whole body like a binder. We left it there for ten days and I was thinking; *Now we've really done something. Laughin' Louie is going to look and think, well, maybe they aren't so stupid after all. Maybe they are smart. They saved my child. Maybe he'll stop laughing and listen. And he might even be grateful we saved his little girl.*

The next day he came by and wanted a pot—a certain size—Jack said we didn't have that size and he said, "You never do anything for us. You never give us anything." We were a little surprised. The baby flourished. We cared for this baby for two weeks while her mother lived on our porch and nursed her. We changed her bandages and kept her clean. These people were not from our village. They went home after a couple of weeks. We found out a few months later that the village where Laughin' Louie, his wife, and little baby lived—something terrible must have happened to the water because eight adults and ten children died of dysentery. Laughin' Louie was one of those who died, along with his wife, his little girl, and his brother.

And I knew that now he knew—he knew we were not in fact stupid. He knew that we were right—that our message was true. This is what I had prayed for. *But God, this is not how I wanted him to know.* Now he knows, and he will know for all eternity that we were offering something of value. We weren't so stupid after all.

After months of struggling with this issue, I decided then and there to give this completely to God. How foolish I had been. What freedom washed over me as I truly trusted God. If God wants us to look smart, wonderful. However, if we need to be fools, so be it. This was no longer in my hands, but in the hands of the One who made me and called me. This was one of the hardest lessons I had to learn. I didn't have to prove what I was. I didn't have to worry about what I wasn't. I had simply to present the truth of the gospel and let God do the rest. How great the relief when we finally turn a situation over to God in complete surrender. Then I prayed that God would help me love all these people all the time, even the obnoxious ones.

8

MAMA ALLIGATOR

"Finally, my brothers, rejoice in the Lord!"
PHILIPPIANS 3:1

Nights in the tribe were fun. There were no video games, no TVs, no malls, no restaurants, and no movies to go to, but the nights were fun, nonetheless. Each evening, following tub baths and dinner, we squeezed into the area of the bunk beds. By now, we had screened in a small room, just large enough for the two bunks, a shelf, and the double bed. We didn't have to sleep with nets, as this room was screened and bug-proof. We would light a candle and start with a hymn. We took turns picking the hymns, and that would be the hymn for the week. We found ourselves singing it throughout the day and meditating on the words in bed. How God blessed me with these old hymns. Next we memorized some verses, or a Psalm, or the order of the books of the Bible. Janey, at three, could rattle them off—"Genesis, Exodus, Lebiticus, Numbers, Duderomy, Joshua, Judges, Ruth." We had prayers and discussed the day.

Following our devotions came the story hour. Each night I read for an hour, unless the plot was too exciting and the girls talked me into "just one more chapter." We read *The Chronicles of Narnia, The*

Vinegar Boy, Nancy Drew, and biographies of other missionaries or saints, presidents, and other interesting people. One night while reading *The Vinegar Boy*, I got so emotional and choked up I couldn't read. Jack grabbed the book and started reading. Soon, he too choked up and handed the book to Kerry. We managed to finish that somehow. We read *Hatchet in the Sky*. The vivid descriptions of winter made us shiver even in the jungle. We read of great escapes and starvation, and our stomachs growled. We read of a man catching and roasting a mouse; we weren't that hungry.

One night after we put the kids to bed, we fell into bed ourselves. Tired and happy, we cuddled and kissed, covered with just a sheet. Janey got up and came over to the bed.

"Daddy, what's in you pocket?"

We were momentarily speechless. What should we say to her? Before we could come up with anything, Janey answered her own question.

"Oh, I know, it's you flashlight," and aimlessly wandered back to her bed.

We had good times with the Indians also. One hot Sunday afternoon, we were all sitting on the porch visiting. They were bored, we were bored. I don't recall who came up with the idea, but we decided to make stilts. It's amazing what you can do with a machete. We made two pairs, and Kerry and Lorrie showed them how to walk on them. They all learned quickly. The parents got involved and began making their own stilts. Soon, most of the men and children were walking around the village on stilts of all sizes.

The Indians also loved looking at our View Masters. They pored over the *National Geographic* magazines. They would look at the pictures of other indigenous people, rubbing the paper fondly, tenderly, almost caressing them.

Do all children dare each other to do things? I think, yes. The Guayabero children would put a whole pepper in their mouths and place it in their cheek. Then they would all run around and try to bust the pepper in another's cheek. Occasionally one kid would have his pepper smashed. He would have tears streaming down his face, his mouth burning for several hours, while the rest of them laughed.

We had pineapples planted in the back yard. The children would watch them grow. I would watch them grow. I liked to pick them when they were ripe. Just about the time my pineapples were ready to be picked, the children would bring me a nice pineapple to buy. Then I would look out back, sure enough, my pineapple had disappeared! I would playfully shake my finger at the little thieves and take the pineapple without paying for it and they would run off giggling.

The Guayaberos scraped the land all around their houses so there was no growth, no grass, no weeds, etc. This was to discourage snakes coming into the houses. They did this around our house. In the rainy season, June, July, and August, because the ground around Macuare is very flat, the rain falls and stays pooled and the ground gets very slick.

Washing clothes in the rainy season presented challenges. The girls had a system. They started by using an old washboard propped up in a galvanized tub filled with water. They would scrub and scrub. Between the two tubs were rollers that they fed the wash through to squeeze out excess water. Joy and Janey handed the clothes to me and I would hang them on the line. Sheets and towels were more difficult than clothes. They were heavy and bulky. The wringer did little good. Usually we just coiled them tight, a person on each end. More than once, as I walked to the line to hang them up, I slipped on the slick mud. Down I went with all the clean clothes flying everywhere, falling in the mud. What's there to do but laugh and start over? Sorry girls. This needs to be redone. Clothes hanging on the line might stay there a week, getting rained on many days before they actually dried. Today, my heart cannot help itself—when I push the little start button on my beautiful Amana washing machine, it gives a little flutter. By the time I push the start button on my beautiful, pristine, white, automatic dryer, my heart leaps for joy.

Mango trees surrounded our yard. Around March of each year, they would be loaded with mangos. All this sap brought bees. One day, Janey and Joy were out playing under the trees and Janey got stung on her left ear. Her ear was soon very swollen and she looked like Dumbo. This might have been funny had it not been so serious. Soon she was having trouble breathing. We sat up with her most of the night, praying to God for her life. Once again, God was faithful. Janey made a full recovery. For several days, her enormous ear amused the village. We were just grateful she was still with us.

I, too, had serious allergies. They were a mystery—maybe mold, maybe mangos, who knows? One night my eyes started swelling, and as my throat started swelling, I found I couldn't breathe easily. I struggled for air most of the night. It was very frightening. By the next day, I couldn't get my eyes open. Jack called Lomalinda and asked for a plane to come pick me up. He told the people that my eyes were swollen. Kerry took over, fixing breakfast, packing what things we needed at the base, getting her three little sisters dressed and ready. The girls would all go in with me. Jim Lush brought the plane. As I was led to the plane, I could hear the people saying, "It's true. There are no eyes!"

Once we were airborne, Kerry relaxed, her responsibilities suspended for the moment, she promptly threw up. We landed at Lomalinda and people began whispering around me. Did they think I was deaf as well as blind? I could hear Ron McIntosh close to me.

"Nice to see you, Ron," I kidded. Everyone laughed. That broke the ice.

The seriousness of the attack forced us to seek medical attention in the United States. In September, Jack went back to Macuare and the girls and I traveled to North Carolina and moved in with Grandma Charlotte in Waxhaw at the JAARS Center. The girls rode the school bus each morning and I picked them up in the afternoon. Janey wasn't in kindergarten yet. After numerous tests, doctors decided that I was allergic to almost everything. That wasn't very helpful, but I did get epinephrine and instructions on how to give myself a shot if and when this happened again. I taught Kerry and Lorrie how to give me an injection, and Jack was a pro at giving shots by now.

We missed Jack. He was to come home just before Christmas. We would stay through the holidays, and then return to Colombia after the first of the year. One day I took Janey to the finance office and the lady leaned over the counter and asked her, "Who's coming to town?"

"Daddy"

"No, Santa Claus. Santa Claus is coming to town."

"Who's that?" Janey asked.

How easy it was to shield our children from the influences of the world. No one at Lomalinda ever mentioned Santa Claus. We all had birthday cakes and sang *Happy Birthday* to Jesus. My children grew up thinking this was the norm, that this is what everyone did. How little did they know. There was a time that I thought this isolation from the world was a good thing. Then came a time that I thought some exposure might have been beneficial for them.

Jack finally arrived. What a reunion! How wonderful to all be together again. We celebrated a wonderful Christmas. In early January, we left and headed back to the field. We got the older girls settled in at the home of our neighbors, dear friends and prayer partners, Harold and Ellen Beaty at Lomalinda, unpacked from the trip to the States, packed for the trip to Macuare, and flew to the village.

We were making progress in language learning. The Indians had begun to trust us. Life was good. Our center had a farm where they experimented with local crops and different livestock. They offered courses to Indians in the villages. The Guayaberos were hunters and gatherers. Each year their land shrunk as Colombians settled the surrounding area. Long-term survival meant learning a new way of life. We thought perhaps if they had large fields of cacao trees they could harvest each year; at least they would have a cash crop. Besides, little cacao beans meant chocolate and I love chocolate. In spring, an instructor came to give the people a course. He came with hundreds of cacao seedlings. He showed the people how to clear the land. Cacao trees can live under large trees and grow in the shade, so they cleared only the underbrush. Following two weeks of instructing, clearing, and planting, the instructor left with the promise he would return the following year at harvest time to give instructions for harvesting, fermentation, drying, and roasting.

The fields were neglected. Most of the saplings died, many buried under new growth of vines and weeds. The rainfall was less than usual and the results of the crop were disappointing. The instructor returned and scolded the people on their lack of care. At one point he said, "Do you know why the plants died?"

Our people were smart. They all knew why the plants died.

"Yes," they proudly responded. "Because it hasn't rained!"

Moises was standing next to Jack.

"Do you know why it didn't rain?' he asked.

"No, why?"

"Because we have been eating alligator and Mama Alligator is mad at us for eating up all her young. Mama Alligator controls the water, the rains, and the rivers."

We started having tremors, small quakings of the earth. We heard the people talking. They knew they must stop eating alligators. Mama was really angry. So it was agreed; they would all stop. Sure enough, the tremors stopped.

For the Indians to share this information with us meant a great deal. This was a turning point in our relationship with them and from this time forward, they shared many taboos, folklore, and just plain ol' gossip with us.

Our house in Macuare

Thirteen year olds with their new babies

Our family in front of airplane in Macuare

Young boy with bow and arrow he made himself

Transportation at Lomalinda

Young boy with his bow and arrow

Rachel

Moises and Mer with some of their daughters

Getting mail on flight into Macuare

Little girls outside our home—Carlotta is the little one in front row, lower right

Vicente's wife with Janey

Little boys

Lorrie at our well

Kids playing on our porch

9

EYEBROWS

//

"Taking the five loaves and the two
fish and looking up to heaven,
he gave thanks and broke the loaves."
MARK 6:41

O ur shortwave radio was a great comfort. We had to check in two days a week, but we could call in anytime if we needed anything. On Sundays the schedule was different. They would be on standby from 8:00 to 9:00 a.m. and 2:00 to 3:00 p.m. only. One Sunday, the people were having their town meeting in the village and Alberto was preaching. I was sitting on a log on the women's side and Jack was on the other side with the men. Children weren't required to attend these meetings and were allowed to run and play. Close to the end of the service, Alberto's little daughter, Leonore, (about six or seven years old) came up to Alberto and began crying, "Daddy, Daddy, ach, ach, ach…"

He was very proud and wouldn't stop preaching and shoved her to the side. She went to her uncle Felipe and he pulled her hand away. When he pulled her arm, I could see that the arm wasn't straight. It zigzagged. I looked at my watch and it was one minute to 9:00! I shouted,

"Jack, her arm is broken. You get her. I'm going to run home to turn on the radio."

I went tearing back to the house and grabbed the radio and started shouting, "Lomalinda, Lomalinda, Macuare, Macuare!"

Usually I turned it on and waited politely to see if anybody was talking, as I didn't want to interrupt, but today I just wanted to be sure they didn't sign off. We needed to talk to the doctor. Paul Closious was still on standby.

"Can you wait Macuare? I'm talking too... over."

"Sure, just don't sign off! Over."

I waited and waited and finally, they finished chatting and I told Paul I had a medical emergency and needed the doctor.

"Why didn't you tell me that? Over."

"You asked me to wait. Over."

Even fellow missionaries, godly as they are, can be frustrating.

By the time Dr. Altig got on the radio, Jack was home with Leonore, followed by the whole village. We laid her down on the porch, her head in Lorrie's lap. Lorrie kept rubbing her forehead with a wet washrag. That morning in my devotions I read about our efforts. Sometimes, they are just feeble efforts. God takes our feeble efforts and then blesses them, like the little boy who had five loaves and two fish. That lunch looked small considering all the hungry people. But that tiny lunch, when given to Jesus, was multiplied to feed thousands. When I finished reading this devotion, I thought, *that's neat*, but promptly forgot all about it. Well, I'd never seen a broken arm, let alone tried to set one. With Leonore screaming at the top of her lungs, I leaned over, took her upper arm in my hands, Jack took her wrist, and we began pulling opposite each other. I thought to myself, *God, of all the feeble things anybody has ever done, this has got to be the feeblest!*

I knew that God, just as He had done with the five small loaves and two fish, could take our feeble efforts, multiply them, and turn them into something good. Kerry was on the radio with Dr. Altig. He stayed with us four hours that Sunday afternoon, giving us encouragement and directions to check for this, check for that, how to make a splint etc., etc. What a team. The bamboo splint we made was overkill. One side of her body was so heavily weighed down, she limped as she walked. Six weeks later, we removed the splint and to our delight, her arm was perfect. Thanks be to God. He had taken our feeble efforts and brought us success. With God as our partner, all things are possible.

I learned something else that day. I learned why we have eyebrows! When I was a little kid, I used to wonder why we had eyebrows. When I became a Christian, I came to believe God had a purpose for everything He'd created. The day Leonore broke her arm was very hot. I was very nervous and soon big drops of sweat began rolling down my forehead. They hit my eyebrows and detoured off to the side of my face. As we leaned over Leonore, I said to Jack, "I just figured out why we have eyebrows."

"I think you've flipped! Just keep pulling!"

"No, really. Just think how much God has done for us. We don't have any idea how much He's done for us. For one thing, we don't have salty sweat stinging our eyes because we have eyebrows!"

Jack rolled his eyes and continued the attempt to set her arm—our feeble effort given to God.

10

TWENTY-FOUR
MATURE OXEN

"No one who puts his hand to the plow and looks
back is fit for service in the kingdom of God."
LUKE 9:62

We are told to count the cost of following Jesus. Years before, as I sat in my centrally air conditioned (or heated depending on the season), wall-to-wall carpeted home that was fully equipped with running water, two inside bathrooms, electricity, washer/dryer, refrigerator with ice dispenser, two televisions, and a two-car garage with two cars sitting inside, these things, I'm ashamed to admit, were the things that came to my mind as I considered the cost. How could I possibly have counted the cost? I lived in luxury and comfort, and being far too focused on material things, believed these would be my sacrificial offerings.

In my life, I have had numerous misconceptions. Beliefs and ideas I thought to be one way turned out not to be so. Knowledge and experience often revealed the very opposite to be true. And so, as understanding dawned in my head, I would say, "Oh." My life has been one lesson after another— a series of things seen from God's perspective; a series of misconceptions, corrected—a series of "Ohs."

I have observed that other people have common misconceptions also. Misconceptions such as missionaries are more spiritual than most Christians. Missionaries are so spiritual, they can't be bothered with what kind of clothes they wear. They won't notice and even if they do, won't care if the tea bag has been used. I had the common misconception missionaries were the happiest people on earth, and that once we became missionaries, we would live happily ever after. These misconceived ideas gave me no reliable basis for counting the costs of following Christ anywhere, let alone to the mission field.

So, just what is it God wants from us? What does it mean to count the cost? What does it mean to put your hand on the plow and not look back? I Kings 19:19 and 20 tells us that Elisha wanted to go with Elijah, but said, "Let me go back and kiss my mother and father goodbye." He went back and killed his twelve pair of oxen, every single one of them. It is no small task to kill twenty-four fully mature oxen. You can be sure he knew the cost. Talk about burning your bridges! And speaking of burning, he then burned the plowing equipment and used it to barbecue the meat, which he gave the people to eat. Elisha never said, "Well, I'll loan my teams to my good friend to use while I'm gone. Then if it doesn't work out with Elijah, I can always return home, retrieve my oxen, and begin farming again." No. He killed them *all.* These twenty-four mature oxen represented all Elijah had, everything. He burned the plow. He made it impossible to return to the life he once knew! This demonstrated full commitment. This was a loud statement of faith. I think this is what God wants. No matter what the cost, we commit to follow Him. No wishy washy, I'll try it for a while, see what happens, and then decide. No, He wants us to slaughter everything from our previous life and follow Him, no strings attached, no turning back.

Did I miss my air conditioning? Definitely. Did I miss indoor plumbing? Absolutely. Were these the things I missed the most? No. And again I say, no. What, then, are the sacrifices a missionary makes? What were my twenty-four mature oxen?

First and foremost, missionaries give up time with their extended families. In Colombia, Thanksgiving is not a holiday, so we squeezed in a private celebration in the evening or the next weekend. We knew our families back home were gathered in large groups enjoying each other, watching football games together, and eating turkey and cranberry relish. We knew we were missing out on some great fun.

Shortly after one such Thanksgiving, I began singing "White Christmas" and dreaming of the Christmases in Michigan. This time of year is the beginning of Colombia's dry season. They practice slash and burn agriculture, and soon after the onset of the hot dry winds, Colombians set their fields on fire. The end result is black hills as far as you can see and a smoky, hazy atmosphere that stings your eyes and nose. So, I'm dreaming of a white Christmas surrounded by black hills. One day, while living at Lomalinda, I was cruising home from the commissary with Kerry on the back of my motorcycle, looking at the ugly charred remains of grass, longing for snow-covered branches of tall, stately pine trees when Kerry piped up, "It's beginning to look like Christmas! Isn't it neat?"

Out of the mouth of babes, God sometimes gently nudges us to focus on our blessings. *Oh Lord, forgive me, help me to think of the blessings I have instead of what's missing.*

And still, I did miss much. My Grandma Redman died. Going to her funeral was out of the question. I grieved alone. My youngest sister, Janey, got married. She made a beautiful bride, I'm told, but I wasn't there. My parents moved twice and lived in homes I never saw. Nephews and nieces were born, grew, walked, and talked before I met them. All the missionaries at Lomalinda knew the ache for our families we left behind. We filled the void by becoming surrogate families to each other. As a result, many strong bonds were formed. We celebrated holidays and birthdays together. We invited the singles. No one was ever alone on a holiday.

The second biggest sacrifice for most missionaries is their health. Not only are there a great new variety of ailments, parasites, and diseases, the health care is often at a great distance and substandard. Lorrie and I didn't have the best teeth. In the mid-seventies, the dentistry in Bogotá was poor. No modern equipment to help ease the pain there. All of the work I had done needed to be repeated years later, and as a result, I have thirteen crowns. Lorrie too, has had major dental work done repairing poor work or lack of work. I believe along with my new body, I'm going to get a new set of teeth—and I'm not talking dentures!

Lorrie had a congenital knee problem and her kneecaps would dislocate periodically. This was extremely painful and remained painful for several days. I learned how to straighten her leg and with the palm of my hand whack the kneecap back in place while she screamed. She spent many months in a wheelchair with fluid on her knee. She has a twelve-inch long scar on both knees from numerous surgeries. After the surgery in South America didn't fix the problem, we scheduled to have it repeated in the United States while on a furlough. Lorrie's Dallas doctor had operated on several of the Dallas Cowboys, which moved him up the ladder for Lorrie. She then wore casts that extended from her crotch to her ankles. This presented numerous challenges; for example, to wash her hair, I laid her on the kitchen counter on her back, head hanging in the sink.

The worst day of her six-week ordeal occurred on a Sunday. We were visiting a supporting church and planning to return to Dallas the following week. The service was over and we were strolling across the churchyard when she started yelling. We ran to her and found she had stepped in a bed of fire ants and they were halfway up her legs inside her casts! With the help of some church members, we laid her down and poured rubbing alcohol into the casts. Following a wonderful Sunday lunch with some of the church members, we took a Greyhound Bus back to Dallas. They requested we store the crutches below with the luggage. When we arrived in Dallas, we found that the crutches had been stolen. How low can one go?

Many of our fellow missionaries got malaria, hepatitis, and various other ailments. Our family was blessed with good health. Of course, the girls and I all got parasites. This included roundworms, whipworms, pinworms, and amoebas. Joy was about eight months old when I found a live, twelve-inch long roundworm in her diaper.

"Call the plane!" I yelled at Jack, "I'm going home!"

He calmed me down. We prayed. We treated Joy. We stayed.

Jack never seemed to be afflicted by parasites; a fact that gave him great pride. He attributed this to his efficient hand washing techniques, which irked me. I argued that it had more to do with the fact that he spent his days working in his office with Moises or Vicente while the girls and I mixed, played, and ate with the entire village. Then, one evening, Jack wanted me to look at his back; he thought he might be getting a boil, and yes, right there in the middle of his back was a round, red welt. We decided to keep an eye on it. Daily it grew more tender and a bit larger. One evening, I had the flashlight pointed right at it and could see a small hole and then, right before my very eyes, out popped a tiny head! Before I could react, it pulled back inside.

I screeched, "Ugh! It's a worm! Gross! You have a worm!"

Sure enough, a fly had managed to lay an egg right in the middle of Jack's back. We were planning to return to Lomalinda in about a week, so Dr. Altig recommended we leave it for him to extract. I tried without success not to enjoy this moment. I guess superb hand washing techniques didn't rule out parasites of the back.

I'm at the other end of my life now, and looking back, I have yet another moment of understanding, another "Oh," a new perspective. Was there really a cost to following Jesus? Did I really make any sacrifices? The joy of the years of being God's child has been so great, the work so rewarding, the "oh the places you'll go" have been so interesting, the experiences so vast, it appears after all, there was no cost to me, only gain.

11

FURLOUGH

///

*"Foxes have holes and birds of the air have nests
but the Son of man has no place to lay his head."*

MATTHEW 8:20

A book could be written entitled *Missionaries on Furlough*. We have shared many laughs with fellow missionaries about our unusual, often hilarious experiences as we make our ways back into the culture of the great United States. I had experienced a degree of culture shock moving to South America. This was expected and we had prepared ourselves as best we could for the transition. Returning to the wonderful USA, however, threw all of us into a culture shock that we didn't expect.

The fast pace of American culture brings rapid change. While we were living in a laid back, I'll do it tomorrow, there's no rush atmosphere, people in America were very busy expanding, developing, inventing, and multiplying. The choice of cereal alone can causes heart palpitations.

We flew into Miami for a short furlough and were planning to buy a car there, drive to Orlando, take the girls to Disney World, and then proceed to North Carolina to visit with Grandma Charlotte. The Wycliffe staff working in Miami picked us up at the airport and took us to our motel. I *could not* figure out how to open the door. Just where had they hidden the handle? Our friendly chauffeurs soon pointed out its location, neatly tucked into the design of the armrest. Clever, but invisible. Later that day, they pointed us in the direction of a reputable used car dealer and loaned us a car to drive there. We left the girls at the motel watching TV and headed off to buy the car. We found the Christian car dealer, bought a station wagon, and headed home. Jack would drive our new used car and I was to follow him in the office car. Somewhere amid road construction and red lights, I lost sight of my lead car and took a wrong turn. I hadn't driven a car in five years. It seemed like everyone was driving 90 mph and I wanted to drive 30 mph. I was lost and my palms were sweating.

I passed a sign that read *Orlando 218 miles.* About fifteen minutes later, it began to rain. I had no idea how to turn on the windshield wipers. The car windows began to steam up, but the dashboard knobs were a mystery to me. Then I saw a sign that read *Orlando 195 miles.* Why, I asked myself, was Orlando getting closer? Things didn't add up. I decided to pull off and call the office. At the gas station, to my dismay, I learned that call would be long distance. Having been in Florida less than six hours, I had no U.S. currency. I asked the attendant if he could point me in the direction of Miami. He looked at me as if to say, "Where have you been living? In the jungle or something?" Little did he know.

I got back in the car, figured out the defrost thing, got the wipers up and wiping, said a prayer asking God for help, and pulled back on the freeway heading back in the direction I had just come. Three hours later, I arrived safely back at our motel. My worried family, relieved to see me, demanded to know where I'd been.

"Well, I'm not exactly sure," was my feeble answer.

The next day, Lorrie and I went to gas up the new car. We pulled up at the station, but no friendly gas attendant came out to greet us. The pump said, "Self." What in the world did that mean? The pump would pump for us? We got out. Another car pulled out and the driver jumped out and opened his gas tank and began pumping gas himself. We watched him closely. What was this? When did this happen? Slowly it began to dawn on me, self meant self-service—you do it yourself. *Okay, I thought, we can do this, just unscrew the gas cap.* But, alas, we couldn't find it. We looked first on one side, then on the other, then danced and moved around the car, trying desperately not to look foolish. We didn't manage to find the cap, so we got back in the car and burst into gales of laughter. We later learned that it was hidden neatly under the license plate of all places.

We had a lovely visit with Grandma Charlotte, then headed to Dallas.

Wycliffe has a center in Duncanville, which is south of Dallas, and my folks lived in North Dallas. As soon as we got settled into temporary housing, I took off with the girls to go visit my mom and dad. We pulled on the North Dallas Toll Road and I tossed my purse into the back seat and asked the girls to get me two quarters. I had learned my lesson, and had plenty of good old U.S. currency. The girls poured out the change into their hands and began staring at the coins.

"Mom, which one is a quarter?"

Oh boy, I thought, *we have lots to teach these girls.* Kerry then said that Frontage Road must be the longest road in the United States as we saw signs for this road everywhere.

We decided that we would do some deputation while home. This is the fundraising part of missions, and while it was my least favorite job, we did meet lots of interesting, wonderful, generous, and godly people while doing it. Wycliffe Associates has a roster of places that will house missionaries while traveling on furlough. We had never done this and with four small children, I questioned the wisdom, but for lack of funds, we went this route. We had supporters from Texas all the way to Michigan. We began the drive, staying with a different family each night. In Ohio, we woke up to a beautiful snowfall. The girls ran outside, laughing, jumping, and trying to make snowballs, all except Kerry. She stood alone, dejected, looking very sad. I walked over to her.

"What's wrong, honey?" I asked her.

"Mom, these flakes are so small. The ones we make in Colombia are this big."

She held up her hands to indicate a snowflake about 8x8 inches, and I realized the ones they cut out of folded paper had misled her into thinking that they were actually that size. What a disappointment for a little girl's first sight of snow.

We stayed with many kind, generous people who opened their homes to us, fed us fabulous meals, and treated us like family. One family even took us riding on their snow machines after lending us snow pants and jackets. What fun to spend the day sliding down a hill, building snowmen, and riding on snowmobiles.

We did have a most embarrassing moment during one of these visits. The lady of the house and two teenage children welcomed us. We didn't meet the husband. The next morning at breakfast, he came formally to the table, introduced himself, pulled out a Bible, and announced that we would now have our daily devotions. His two teenagers giggled and squirmed. Unfortunately, it was quite obvious they didn't do this often. He read from Scripture then told us he wanted the kids to each recite their favorite memory verse. He looked at his oldest daughter and she came up with nothing. I felt sorry for her as she was put on the spot and drew a blank. I didn't have long to worry about her though, as I wondered how my girls would perform under this kind of pressure. We had memorized numerous verses and passages, but would they remember any of them here and now? Working his way around the table, his eyes then landed on Lorrie. She looked at me, then at her dad, and then, she too drew a blank. The tension mounted. Our host was getting frustrated. All eyes turned to twelve-year-old Kerry, who clearly, loudly, and perfectly recited, "The heart is deceitful above all things and desperately wicked; Who can know it?" (Jeremiah 17:9 KJV).

Did I laugh? Did I cry? Did I crawl under the table? I honestly don't remember. I do know that our host got up from the table, walked from the room, and wasn't seen again.

As I tucked the girls in bed that night, I said to Kerry, "Surely, that's not your favorite verse, is it?"

"No, but Mom, it was the only one I could think of at the moment."

At this moment, I was rather eager to end our furlough. I was out of my comfort zone and ready to be home. Home to Colombia. We had a few more weeks of speaking engagements, then the farewells to friends and family before getting on the plane. How different this trip was from our first. This time there was no fear of the unknown. All of us eagerly hopped on the plane.

12

THE WITCH DOCTOR

"For our struggle is not against flesh and blood,
but against the rulers, against the authorities,
against the powers of this dark world and against
the spiritual forces of evil in the heavenly realms."

EPHESIANS 6:12

Once again we were back in beautiful Colombia. Our girls had always looked forward to going to the tribe. They had friends and enjoyed being in the village. That was all about to change. Kerry was now thirteen, and Lorrie eleven. We flew to Macuare and got off the plane. Their friends came to greet us. They were all carrying their new babies! What a shock. Now the young boys started looking at Kerry and Lorrie as marriage material, and the young girls, their old friends, were busy taking care of their babies. This tribal stay turned out to be fairly boring for Kerry and Lorrie, so we decided next time we would leave them at the center, at least during school. I had determined I would homeschool them until high school graduation, but that wasn't to be.

Wanting to celebrate the birth of our Lord with other Christians, we returned to Lomalinda sometime in November. After Christmas, we got Kerry and Lorrie settled in the children's home and took the younger girls back to the village. Leaving the girls behind was very difficult for me. I missed them terribly.

Each Saturday, we got fifteen minutes to talk to Kerry and Lorrie on the shortwave radio. During the week, I would make a list of the things I wanted to tell them. They did the same thing. Early Saturday we turned on the radio and listened to all the translators talk to their children. Some kids had nothing to say.

"How are you? Over."

"Fine. Over."

"How was your week? Over."

"Fine. Over."

"How is school? Over."

"Good. Over."

This wasn't the case with the Keels women. From start to finish, we talked as fast as we could and still never really finished. After these talks, I would be very sad for several hours. I really missed my girls. They always sounded like they were having a good time. Many years later, Joy, however, confessed to me that she cried herself to sleep in the children's home almost every night.

While we had been celebrating the birth of our Lord at Lomalinda, the Guayaberos had been celebrating too. Moises and some other men had been drinking and a fight ensued. Moises had two large machete cuts—one on the lower arm that had severed all muscles, and one on his shoulder. His right hand hung, useless, from his wrist. Not only did he have no sons, he now had no right hand. When we arrived in early January, he told us that he wanted to start working with us, helping us learn the language, and that way, he could at least make a little money. Jack took him up on the offer. Vicente came in the mornings and Moises in the afternoons. Moises was quite a bit smarter than Vicente and we made more progress on the language analysis.

Jack began to translate various passages and a new hurdle emerged. He was through and through a pure perfectionist. Maybe this came from his architectural training, where everything had to be exact. Plans only a few inches off could mean disaster for a large building project. Bible translation, on the other hand, is not an exact science. The meanings of words can resemble areas almost cloud-like in nature with ill-defined borders overlapping with other ill-defined borders. As a result, decisions of word choice have to be made. Two words might work well, but which would work better? Jack would translate a verse or passage and be satisfied with it, and then later, doubts would creep in. Maybe that other word would have been better, conveyed the meaning better. After hours of reflection, he would change the translation and again be satisfied. No sooner had this been accomplished than new doubts cropped up and the verse or passage once again would be reworked, revised, reworded.

Over the many years we worked with the Guayaberos, Jack would translate and complete only *The Life of Christ*, a synopsis of the Gospels and Acts. He had a rough draft of the *Old Testament Summary* that was never finished. These are fairly factual historical accounts lending themselves more easily to translations than the epistles, which deal with philosophies, concepts, intangible doctrines, and tenets that present a great many problems. Still, Jack was never happy with these two books and determined that sometime later, when he had the time, both these works would yet again be revised.

It was difficult, no—impossible, for me to understand the depths of frustration Jack felt as he struggled for perfection. The standard he set for himself would always be slightly out of reach and be as unobtainable as it was impracticable. He was dissatisfied with his work, thinking for the most part it was substandard, below par, not publishable. Self doubts as pesky gnats in the village began to assail him. *I can't do this. Whatever made me think I could translate God's Word? How could I ever think the end result would be the inspired living word of God when I know that it's filled with these peevish errors, these inferior phrases, these incomplete thoughts?* The work that should have been rewarding and fulfilling now, on the contrary, left him feeling totally inadequate and frustrated. I, too, felt inadequate as how to help him—my words of advice not having the desired effect, I kept my council to myself and silently prayed.

On the other hand, it was very rewarding to know that we were finally winning their trust. As a result, they began to reveal more of their oral traditions. Since we had studied anthropology, I had visions of writing a dissertation, or at least a thesis, on these traditions. I soon learned that most were X-rated stories I wouldn't want to publish.

There was a widespread belief among the Guayaberos that when the last Guayabero dies, the burning logs of the moon and sun will die and the world will cease to exist. That is why we were sent to work with them—to insure their continuity. The burning logs were part of a legend. A woman had sex with a tree, got pregnant, and gave birth to a son she called Wheempt. When Wheempt was a teenager, he was rebellious, as most teens are. One day, his rebelliousness led to a huge argument. Mom threw him out, into the sky. He grabbed part of her fire, some of her burning logs, and he flew through the heavens carrying these logs. He is now the sun and the moon. When Wheempt is lying down, that is the moon. When Wheempt is sitting straight up, he is the sun and it is high noon.

The Guayaberos held the belief that the creator of the universe was a god named Kuwoy, and upon death, the spirit of the deceased joins Kuwoy in his land down below. Many of the Indians prayed to Kuwoy, feared him, and could recollect moments when they spoke to him directly and audibly heard back from him. These were usually during the times that the Guayaberos were under the influence of the powerful drug, *yopo* that was commonly used among the Indians.

As Jack began work on *The Life of Christ* with Vicente and Moises, they began to have many questions about God and Jesus. Everything we told them they believed, but they didn't give up any of their old beliefs. Moises said, "Sure, I believe in God. I also believe in Satan. I believe Satan has more power than God."

One or two nights a month, the Guayaberos held ceremonies in which they used *yopo*. Late at night, we could hear them chanting. This chanting was eerie, haunting, frightening, and lasted several hours. A few times, Jack walked to the village during the ceremony. They stopped chanting and dancing and just stood there, frozen. No one spoke. No one moved. After ten or fifteen minutes, Jack turned around and came home. The chanting and dancing resumed. The next day, however, they were eager to talk about it. They explained that when they take this *yopo*, they go down under—their spirit goes down under—and they can communicate with their loved ones who have died; they also communicate with Kuwoy. They say Kuwoy is the creator of the universe.

Vicente said to Jack one day, "I'm mixed up. You tell me about Jesus. You tell me about God and I believe you. You wouldn't lie. Yet, when we take *yopo*, we go down under and we see Kuwoy. The last time I did this, I asked Kuwoy, 'Would you tell me about Jesus?' and Kuwoy said, 'There is no Jesus. Look around you. Do you see Jesus? Do you see God?' And I had to say, 'No, I don't see Jesus. I don't see God.' Then Kuwoy said, 'Well, all you see is all there is. Do you see me?' Well, of course I saw him. I was talking to him. Then Kuwoy said, 'Well, I'm all there is. Just look around you. This is all there is. This is the place where all the Guayaberos have come when they died and this is the place where you too will come.'"

Moises also had many questions—"Now tell me again. How do God and Jesus fit in with Kuwoy? If God is who you say He is, who is Kuwoy?"

We actually thought Kuwoy was Satan, or at least a demon. We were uncertain what to tell the people about Kuwoy. We planned to just keep holding up the truth—just holding up Jesus.

Most cultures believe in life after death; the Guayaberos were no exception. They believed that when you die, your spirit goes down to live with Kuwoy. In order for this to happen, a door has to open. For instance, when a child dies, the door is opened briefly, just a small way, and the child slips in. A chief or more influential adult, however, will put up some resistance, so the door has to be opened wider and for a longer period of time. Some of the spirits that are already with Kuwoy may be standing near the door on the inside. While the door is open to let in the newly deceased, these spirits can and do escape. These escaped spirits are free to roam for a few days—up to a week—then they must go back. We never learned why or how they were impelled to return, just that they were.

These spirits may be your relatives. If you were mean to them, unfair to them, stole from them, slept with their wives, etc, these spirits that escaped could torment you. They did this by setting your house on fire, making your firewood so wet you couldn't start a fire, making a child sick, or scaring away a wild tapir or boar just when you are about to throw a spear at it. This belief often controls the wailing after death. The wailing that follows the death of a child is genuine. The wailing following an adult may or may not be genuine. The death of a powerful person causes the whole village to wail. They wail over and around the corpse for two full days. The wailing is continuous. The people take turns, everyone trying to be louder than the next, thinking the dead one can hear and be pleased, hoping that if he ever escapes, he will remember this and not torment them.

At the end of the second day, the dead person is buried. No ceremony is involved with the burial. The person in his hammock is tied to a pole, carried to the burial grounds, and put in a hole. No words are spoken. A bow and arrow or spear is buried with a man to help him on his journey. This is when the door is opened. By this time, most of the people outside the immediate family have already removed themselves from the vicinity, running far off to their fields so they won't be nearby if spirits escape. Escaping spirits sound like wind, so if there is a breeze when the person is put into the ground, you know that at least a few spirits are moving. One can only hope that during the dead person's life, you were civil and have not offended him or her and if you did, your wailing was sufficient to appease the spirit.

One day, two men came into our village carrying a man. He was in his hammock tied to a pole and he swung back and forth as they walked. We were to learn three things about this man. First, he was the brother of the two men who carried him. Second, he was very ill, having been in a coma for two days. Finally, he was the most powerful Guayabero witch doctor. Although he had never lived in Macuare, every person in Macuare knew of him. All feared him. The brothers had brought him to us to cure. As he was in a coma, we couldn't discuss his symptoms. We knew the obvious—he had an elevated temperature and pulse, and he was in a coma. We gave him a shot of penicillin. We prayed. The people in our village told us he better recover. If not, he would be angry with us for all eternity.

In the two days he hung on our porch in his hammock, he never regained consciousness, he wasn't able to eat or drink, and his kidneys didn't function. We knew it was just a matter of time. Toward the end of the second day, he died. The people began coming to wail. The next day, people from neighboring villages came to wail. Even a few people from another tribe came to wail. What a celebrity! We got very little sleep during these days, as he was still hanging on our porch. We told the brothers we were very sorry for their loss, we had done all we could. They were angry. The only words they spoke to us were, "You will get what's coming to you."

At the end of the wailing, the two brothers got up and said, "Enough—we bury him now!"

There was a mass exodus, a fleeing—people grabbling kids, dogs, and belongings and running, actually running. It was very rare to see a Guayabero run. Felipe told us they were heading for the river. He invited us, urged us, to come along with him and his family. We, of all people, wouldn't be safe. We told him our God was able to protect us and we would stay. Within minutes the village was deserted. A ghost town. The village had never been silent. Now there was this deafening silence, an eerie silence—not even a dog barked. This lasted an hour, during which time we prayed and sang a couple of hymns. Even though they were very young, Joy and Janey sensed things were not normal.

Just after sundown, a breeze started. It gathered strength. Soon, our house was swaying back and forth. As the gale picked up, trees bent almost to the ground. Never had we known such a strong wind, not even in the storms. I thought of the Indians huddled on the beach, only a few miles away, terrified, thinking many spirits had escaped.

We, on the other hand, experienced peace. The strong wind reminded me of God's strength and power. Thoughts of John 3:8 came to my mind, "The wind blows wherever it pleases. You hear its sound, but you cannot tell where it comes from or where it is going." What words of comfort. I repeated them over and over; out loud and to myself.

What a comfort to know the security of belonging to a loving God, the great Shepherd, to know nothing can separate you from the love of God; nothing can torment you while you remain in Him. When you dwell in the shelter of the Most High, you rest in the shadow of the Almighty (Psalm 91:1). *Oh, Father, may we be witnesses to your shelter and your comfort. May the Guayaberos see that we have peace, not fear.*

The strong winds lasted about forty-five minutes. This humble servant of God offers no explanation. We knew Satan had powers. We had seen too much evidence in the village to believe otherwise. Maybe this was a manifestation of his limited power and he wanted to frighten us away. Was it the Holy Spirit assuring us of His presence, to guide and protect us? Or perhaps, merely nature? A freak weather pattern? Many things we cannot nor will not understand until we see Him face to face. Truly the wind blows wherever it pleases, yet it is who God controls even the wind and the waves.

13

ROSA AND RACHEL

*"Let the little children come to me,
and do not hinder them, for the kingdom
of heaven belongs to such as these."*
MATTHEW 19:14

Alberto and his young wife had a little daughter, Rosa. She was very ill with glandular tuberculosis and had open, oozing sores around her neck. We were heading back to the center for a couple of months and decided to take her with us. She was weak and frail. When she got on the plane, she whimpered, but didn't have enough strength to really protest. At the clinic, a stool specimen revealed she had three different kinds of worms besides the TB. These were easy to treat, but Rosa was stubborn and didn't want to take the medication. It was also determined that Lorrie had whipworm, so Lorrie, with great ceremony, took her pills, swallowing them like it was fun and games; then handed her glass to Rosa, who took the pills with no further complaints. Within weeks, the results were noticeable. She had an appetite and started gaining weight. She had never seen an indoor toilet and kept running outside to the yard. I finally took her into the bathroom and demonstrated how to use a toilet. Though she turned her head in modesty, she spent the afternoon flushing the toilet, watching the water, amazed at this wonderful invention. She never went in the yard again.

We were returning to the tribe soon, but Rosa wasn't ready. Esther Stein, one of the single ladies at the center, a widow, offered to care for her. She had two junior high school kids, Mark and Kathy, and they were eager to have a little sister. She clung to us and cried loudly, strong enough to protest this time. I tried to assure her we would return in two months. My last glimpse of Rosa was Mark restraining her from running at the airplane, tears streaming down her face. Two months later, Mark had become like an older brother to her. She rode everywhere with him on his motorcycle. She would have been content to live with him forever. However, next time we went to the village, she was very healthy and we decided it was time she return. I was concerned that the time at Lomalinda had made her a misfit in her village. How would she adjust? No flushing toilets here. My concerns vanished as I watched her peers grab her and drag her off to play, all of them giggling as children do so well.

Pablo, Alberto's son from his first marriage, had married and had a family. Guayabero women are not supposed to have sexual intercourse after the birth of a baby. This taboo lasted for the first two years of a baby's life. Pablo and his wife, Maria, broke this taboo, as I'm sure most young couples did, and while nursing helps prevent another pregnancy, it is not a foolproof method of birth control. Their youngest child, Rachel, being only about eighteen months old when the new baby came, struggled to live. She had no teeth, there was no formula, no milk, and no baby food, so she began to starve. Once again, we became foster parents of a Guayabero child. Rachel was almost three by the time she came to live with us. She weighed thirteen pounds and was almost comatose. Our new doctor, Dr. Whitney, who had taken over when the Altigs retired, told us she would probably not recover, and even if she did, would never be able to walk.

She looked like a monkey. I bathed her. It was revolting to look at her arms and legs, all skin and bones, no flesh. Following her bath, I wrapped her up in a towel and went to sit in our rocking chair. I sang as I rocked. I was looking out the window and not at her because she didn't look human and I didn't want to look at her. As I sang, I felt a hand, like a claw, touch my face. I looked down at her and asked God to help me love her as He did. I wanted to see her as He saw her, a precious person, not an animal. God is faithful. I grew to love this child as one of my own.

Lorrie took on the challenge. Between us, we fed Rachel, who we had nicknamed Rocky, with an eyedropper several times an hour for the first week. She soon graduated to a baby bottle, then on to bananas. Her highchair was in the kitchen, where she could see all the action. Joy and her friend, Ginnelle Williams, would dance around her and clap and sing. One day, she looked at them, her eyes focused for the first time, and she clapped her little hands together. We were all very excited. She woke up that day, and from then on, she made great strides. She would eat three pieces of toast, four eggs, drink two glasses of milk—all that just for breakfast. She would eat twice what my girls ate. We bought a swing, and as she bounced up and down, pushing with her weak little legs, and those little legs grew strong. We will never forget the day she took her first steps. We owned a video camera by now and recorded these steps. A baby's first steps are always a momentous occasion, but for this child, no words could describe our joy. We witnessed a true miracle. Being three years of age, she too was old enough to appreciate her accomplishment and walked many miles that first day with a smile on her face that never ended.

What a joy she was. Without question, this was our most pleasurable experience the whole time we lived in Colombia. How sad to learn that a few years after she returned to Macuare, this little child who had become a part of our family, who had stolen our hearts, who called me Mama, who the girls wanted us to adopt, had tripped and fallen into a fire, pulling over a big pot of hot soup. She never recovered and died a long and painful death. It broke our hearts.

Should we have adopted her? We questioned ourselves. No, she had parents and siblings, all who wanted her. I thought we had snatched her from the brink of death for a special purpose, that maybe she would grow to love Jesus and become a missionary to her own tribe. Oh yes, I had plans for her. But my plans were not God's plans and knowing God's plans are far superior to my own, I determined just to trust and obey. God loved Rosa more than we had and she was in His care. But oh, how sad we were when we thought of her death.

14

THE RAT AND OTHER
CULINARY DELIGHTS

||||||||||||||||||||||||||||||||||||||||||||||||||||||||||||||||||||||||||||||||||||||||||

"His food was locust and wild honey"

MATTHEW 3:4

As the girls were older, we had long since moved our bed to the loft that had been created when Jack enclosed the bedroom. A ladder led up to this loft. You couldn't stand up in our new bedroom, but at least it was private. The problem of the bats had improved. Instead of hanging over our beds, they were hanging from the rafters over the porch. From our new bedroom, I was eye level with them, and I didn't enjoy their squeaking every night. I asked the Indians to get me a couple of long branches, which we hung from the porch rafters. I attached a rope to these branches and pulled it through to the end of our bed and put a big loop at the end. Whenever I heard the bats, I stuck my foot in this loop and jerked a few times. This caused the branches to swing back and forth and annoy the bats. The bat population started to dwindle. I was a genius.

Jack now had two language helpers, and many years prior, we had determined that he needed an "office." This we had constructed with

99

the help of the Indians. The office was about thirty feet from the house. What a commute. If I needed Jack, I just called. Not on a phone, since we had no phones; I just called out, "Oh, Jack, can you come…?"

I was fixing lunch one day and Joy and Janey were finishing up their schoolwork when Janey said, "Look, Mommy, a mouse!" I glanced up to where she was pointing and sure enough, on a rafter just above my head, sat a big fat rat. We had borrowed a spear from the Indians, and it was handy, so I grabbed it and stuck it in the rat. This didn't kill the rat; it simply caught him in his rear end. He was squirming and squeaking. I was standing with both arms outstretched, hands held high above my head, pushing the spear with all my might, knowing if I let go, he would probably escape. He might even fall on my head. What to do?

"Oh, Jack, can you come? Like, right now! Immediately! We have a situation here!"

Soon I saw Jack, Moises, and his youngest daughter walking toward me. They started to laugh as they quickly assessed the situation. They relieved me of my burden, stabbed the rat with another spear, and Moises grabbed the rat by his tail and handed him to his daughter, telling her, "Take this home to your mother. We'll have it for lunch."

We bought food from the Indians. If they brought us stuff we didn't want or need, we bought it any way. We were afraid if we didn't, they would think we didn't want their food and stop bringing it altogether. As a result, many times we would have two or three stalks of bananas hanging from the rafters in the kitchen.

One time we had five stalks of bananas hanging from three rafters, making my kitchen look more like a farmer's market than a kitchen. The kitchen wasn't enclosed, leaving all this food exposed. Each night for about a week, we had been awakened by a noise that resembled a terrible, bad mannered slurping and munching sound. It baffled us. What could it be? In the morning we would see banana peelings strewed over the table. We thought maybe it was a dog. We often had dogs wandering on the porch, but we couldn't figure how one could get to the bananas. There was nothing left to do but stay up and wait for the culprit. From our upper loft, we squatted with our flashlights and waited. As soon as we heard the noise, we shined our lights down at the table. Nothing! Nothing? How could that be? We were hearing noises. We shined the light at the rafter, and there sat an opossum, eating our bananas. He played dead for a minute as possums are supposed to do, then decided we posed no threat and resumed eating. He actually peeled the bananas and threw the peelings on the table below.

Besides the spear used to catch the rat, we had also borrowed a bow and arrow from the people. This was the plan. I would stand above and shine the light at the opossum and Jack would shoot him from below with an arrow. This bow was about six feet long and the arrows measured five or six feet. Jack loaded the arrow, pulled back on the string, and let it fly. The arrow dropped straight down to the floor. I giggled. He tried again. Again, the arrow dropped to the floor. I giggled some more. I must also mention that I was in my shorty pajamas, mosquitoes were biting me, and I was trying, without success, to swat them without moving the flashlight around. Jack was getting frustrated. The opossum was sitting there eating like we were invisible. One more time, Jack pulled back on the arrow and one more time it dropped to the floor. That was way too much for me. I laughed out loud. Jack hollered, "Would you hold that flashlight still! This is *not* funny!"

Seven times he tried. My giggles had long since turned to uncontrolled howls. Finally, out of great frustration, he took the arrow, walked up to just below the opossum, and thrust the arrow in its rear, sort of like I had done with the rat. This startled the opossum, but didn't kill it. He jumped down, hit the table, jumped over the half wall in the kitchen, and waddled away with a six-foot arrow stuck in his behind. At this point, even Jack saw the humor and we had a good laugh. That night I had trouble getting to sleep. Each time I started to drift off, I pictured Jack, the possum, and the arrows dropping to the floor, and I would start to laugh all over again. We were overjoyed to learn that the Guayaberos didn't eat possums.

Yes, the Indians brought us food and we bought it all. In the dry season, they would go to the river. The river would be down and there would be long stretches of beach. Turtles would dig holes and lay eggs on the beach, and the Indians loved turtles and their eggs. They often caught more turtles than they needed and kept the turtles on their backs for days. The turtles were alive, but suffering. This bothered me, but they had no refrigeration and this way the meat didn't go bad.

There are two ways to fix a turtle. One, you could just throw it on the fire and barbecue the whole thing. One fine day I was visiting with the women and a bunch of little kids had a cooked turtle on a stump and were gathered around pulling off the cooked meat and stuffing it in their mouths. I happened to look down, and there amongst them was Janey.

"It's yum, Mom! Wanna try it?"

No thanks.

The other method was to start cutting the turtle from the shell. This resulted in one long piece of meat—all the appendages, head, and tail in a long string. This is how they usually brought it to me with the instructions I was to put it in boiling water. I did this a few times, but the meat was always gritty. This turtle lived in sand, why wouldn't it be gritty? One time I got the brilliant idea to wash it off and remove the skin *before* I put it in the boiling water. Maybe it wouldn't be so gritty. I laid the piece of meat in a large pan of water and grabbed a foot and started to peel off the skin; the rest of the meat came to life. I screamed. Jack came running from the office. The girls came running from the yard. They all shouted in unison, "What's wrong?"

"That thing! It's alive! It jumped! It moved!" I yelled as I pointed at the supposedly dead turtle lying in the pan of water.

They climbed into the house and I explained what I was trying to do. I demonstrated, picking up one leg, tugging at the skin. And again, the whole thing came alive. We were fascinated. The girls played with it for hours, pulling one leg making another arm move, jerking an arm, causing the head to rear up. Oh, the things we did to amuse ourselves. After this experience, whenever the Indians brought us a turtle, yes, I immediately put it in the pot of boiling water, grit and all.

The Indians ate monkeys; I don't recommend this stringy, tough meat to anyone. The eyes are considered the great delicacies, and how fortunate we were that monkeys are small, agile, and rarely caught. One afternoon, the group of men shot a monkey with an arrow and she fell to the ground, leaving her baby an orphan. The Indians brought us the baby monkey just to show us, but Kerry fell in love with the monkey and pleaded with us to let her keep it. She wanted a pet. We consented. I should have known, but didn't, that baby monkeys had to be fed every few hours like a human child. Many times during the night, I heard Kerry up with her "baby"—feeding it, comforting it, cooing to it. At dawn, this baby starting howling just as the fully mature monkeys do and it was quite a racket. The girls loved petting this creature and tended to his every need.

Bananas were plentiful. Some were a foot long and others, the cherry bananas, were very small, about an inch long. We decided to have a contest. Who could get the most bananas in their mouth? I think Jack won, managing to stuff thirteen in his mouth at once. The older girls were runners up at nine and ten in their little mouths. The bananas hung from the rafters and as they ripened and grew sweeter, they often attracted bees. Lorrie was stung several times around her eyes and eyelids. This swelled her eyes shut. Joy, too, was stung once beyond recognition. Janey, with her serious allergy to bees, sat at the other end of the table, away from the banana stalks.

The Indians loved fried ants. We had never tried these and never really wanted to, but yes, they insisted. We must! These were a true delicacy. One day they brought me a little cloth bag full of ants. These ants were about an inch long. I was told to put a large skillet on the stove and get it very hot, then dump the ants into the skillet. Within minutes, we would have a tasty, crunchy snack. Yum! Yum!

I lit the fire and put on the skillet. I was nervous, anxious, and eager to get this experience behind me. As a result, most unfortunately, I didn't let the skillet get hot enough. I dumped the ants into the skillet, but as the skillet wasn't hot enough, the heat didn't kill them instantly. No! They hit the skillet and starting running. They escaped! There were hundreds of them, crawling out of the skillet, over the stove, out on the counters, then all over the kitchen. The girls and I squealed and swatted to no avail. We, being no match for a thousand big ants, fled the house, leaving the kitchen to fend for itself.

We all loved catfish. The catfish caught in the Guaviare River were three to four feet long. The whiskers measured up to a foot. The Indians usually chopped off what they would eat and brought the rest to us. I guess fishing was good one day, because down the trail came a little boy with a whole catfish.

I think catfish are funny looking, with their flat heads, flat jaws, eyes on either side, and long whiskers sticking out like a cat. Jack had showed me where to chop off the head, so I was confident I could do it. I took the fish out to a flat rock in the back yard, laid it down, and proceeded to give it a whack. The blow forced air out of the gills, making the thing moan like it was alive. Its eye was watching me.

"Excuse me, mister, but I need to cut off your head."

I had a crowd by now, all laughing, of course, and I whacked again, but couldn't get the head severed. Each whack caused the fish to moan.

"Okay, mister, that's enough! Your head is coming off," and with that I struck a blow that Paul Bunyan would have been proud of.

I love going to the supermarkets in the great United States of America. The meat is all nicely wrapped in cellophane. Packaged. Labeled. Dead. No skin. No scales. What pleasures.

15

THE OLD MAN
BESIDE THE ROAD

///

"When times are good, be happy;
but when times are bad, consider:
God has made the one as well as the other."

ECCLESIASTES 7:14

*T*here were rumors of a whooping cough epidemic upriver. We called the center and had a plane bring vaccinations. We decided to vaccinate for all the childhood diseases. We informed the people and told them to spread the word up and down the river. We would inoculate all small children. They just had to show up. We gave them two weeks to spread the word. On the appointed day, the plane flew in and we had hundreds of people there with their children. One inoculation was a live virus, so it had been packed in ice. We took the vials and the Indians took the ice. They had never seen ice! They rubbed it on their skin, they rubbed it on their children, they ate it, and they threw it at each other. I wish I had a video of that afternoon. They acted like they had just won the lottery.

Meanwhile, we organized the kids in a long line. Joy and Janey dipped cotton balls in alcohol and handed these to us. Kerry handed us the syringes. Jack and I each gave shots. Lorrie comforted the babies when we were finished. The children in line began to panic as they saw what was coming and they began to cry. The children who had just been inoculated were crying. The adults were all yelling and throwing ice and laughing. What a cacophony. Later that night, my arm was sore from giving so many injections. The village was quiet, the people having settled for the night, and I smiled again thinking of the fun grown adults had had with ice.

Sunday afternoon and all was peaceful. We were lying in the hammocks, enjoying a nice breeze. The Indians were playing soccer on the airstrip and we could hear an occasional roar. I had just made coffee and we were slowly sipping from our mugs. Suddenly, the whole team came up to the porch. Pablo was walking lopsided, one arm dangling. He had fallen and dislocated his left shoulder. I got out our trusty medical manual. Pablo lay down on the floor. The book said to pull the arm out from the body at about a 45-degree angle. Jack began pulling. Pablo began moaning. I began sweating. I kept reading and Jack kept following my directions—"Slowly, begin to pull harder and harder."

Jack took a drink of coffee.

"How in the world can you drink coffee at a time like this?" I demanded of him.

"This is just a piece of meat. That's all this is. If I allowed myself to think of him as a man, I wouldn't be able to do this. This is just a piece of meat." All this said in English, of course.

I went back to reading.

"Slowly, begin to pull harder and harder. The muscles will lengthen and you will hear a clunk."

Just about the time I read, "Clunk," we heard a loud clunk. Pablo breathed a sigh of relief. I breathed a sigh of relief. Jack took another drink of coffee. We wrapped his arm tightly in an Ace bandage and told him not to use it for a couple of weeks to give it time to heal. Most of the men went back to their soccer game. Pablo sat on the porch and looked at a View Master. Life was good.

Joy began having a toothache. Each day it worsened. It was about time to return to the center anyway, so we packed up and left. I decided to take Joy to Bogotá and do some shopping. The plane took us to Villavicencio. There we would hire a taxi that would take us over the Andes Mountains, the long and dangerous four to five hour trip. That day, there weren't enough taxis, so we had to share one with other people. They were already sitting in the backseat. Joy didn't want to sit by the driver, so I climbed in the middle beside him and she sat by the door.

Up the winding road we went, swerving and curving. At times, out the side window, you could look deep down to a ravine far below, water raging at the bottom. There were no guardrails, just steep banks. It was very scary. High in the mountains, we entered a small town. We rounded a curve and an old man was standing at the side of the road. To our horror, we hit him and watched as he was thrown toward the front windshield, straight at Joy. How terrifying for her. Our driver slammed on his brakes. Everyone jumped out. The man was hurt and moaning.

Our driver told everyone in the backseat to get out. They picked up the man and threw him in the back seat. A policeman got in too. Off we went to the hospital. Where was the hospital? We drove around for a while. Finally, we found the hospital. They were full, so he had to be taken elsewhere. The policeman decided he didn't want to be cramped in the back seat with this injured man, so he told us to get out. We were dropped off on a corner by a bar; the policeman jumped into the front seat, slammed the door, and away they went.

"Hey, what about our suitcase? What about us?"

I looked around. I was lost. Joy was traumatized by what she had seen and was crying softly. *Lord God, help us. Protect us. Guide us.* I asked directions to the bus stop. Yes, they had a bus to Bogotá, but it had just left; there would be another one in four hours. I bought soft drinks. Soft drinks in Colombia always remind me of the verse in Revelation, "So, because you are lukewarm—neither hot nor cold—I am about to spit you out of my mouth" (Revelation 3:16).

That day, however, those lukewarm soft drinks tasted pretty good. As we sat on the bench, waiting for the bus, swatting flies, I tried to calm Joy. The hours passed and soon we were on a bus, headed for Bogotá. All buses and taxis end up in the same terminal. To my great relief, our taxi driver was there, waiting for us with our suitcase. He offered to take us to the group house. I decided, no, I had had enough of him, and caught another cab.

The next day, we went to the dentist and Joy got her tooth fixed. She was still pretty upset by the accident, so we cancelled the plans for shopping and headed home. We took a taxi back to Villavicencio. This trip was uneventful. We were picked up by a JAARS plane, flown to Lomalinda, and very happy to be home safe. I have often wondered what happened to the man we hit. How seriously was he hurt? I will never know. This became one more incident reminding me that life in a third world country can seem cruel and unfair and how fortunate we Americans really are.

16

THE SUMMER OF
THE CHILDREN

//

*"A voice is heard in Ramah, mourning and
great weeping, Rachel weeping for her
children and refusing to be comforted,
because her children are no more."*
JEREMIAH 31:15

Summertime. How different from the summers of my youth—going
to the cottage at the lake, water-skiing, sailing, cousins coming to
visit and share the lake, hamburgers or hotdogs roasting, fires on the
beach, just general goofing off, having fun. Summer in the jungle meant
rainy season, and all of us in the tribe, as the girls had no school. All six of
us piled into the plane to spend the summer in Macuare with the prom-
ise of good times with the Indians and the girls. This would turn out to
be the worst summer we spent at Macuare. The rains always brought
colds, chills, and fever. That summer, the people never got better; they
just kept getting sicker and sicker. We soon had a village full of people
with pneumonia. We had a special flight just to bring penicillin to give

to the Indians. We used a slow acting injection as we could not monitor oral antibiotics for so many people.

Upriver lived an old lady. She was the oldest lady in the tribe and I liked her. We called her Old Lady. She had a cancer on the side of her face that had eaten a hole on one side, but she was healthy except for that. She would often come and sit with me on the porch and talk about her children and grandchildren. Many had died. She told of how the Guayabero tribe used to number in the thousands until a whooping cough epidemic came and killed hundreds, many of her children and grandchildren included. Old Lady was one of the few old people living, because the Guayaberos don't care for their elderly, often allowing them to starve. Old Lady had somehow fended for herself and now was so old everyone shared leftovers with her.

One day, Samuel, her grandson, came to the porch and told me Old Lady was sick. Would I come and give her a shot? She was about five miles upriver at the home of one of her sons. Because of the dangers of traipsing five miles in the jungle, Jack decided he should go. He hiked to the village, carrying more supplies in case he needed them. He returned home several hours later, empty handed. I stayed in Macuare and gave shots most of the afternoon. No wonder they call this the miracle drug. By the next day, many people were up and about. We heard wood being chopped and people stirring, not moaning and groaning as we had for the past week. Within a week almost everyone, including Old Lady, had recovered.

Carlotta

Little Carlotta was still lying in her hammock. She had not wanted a shot and had cried so when I tried to give her one, I decided just to walk to Felipe's house four times a day and give her an oral antibiotic. When she still didn't respond, I decided to go ahead and give her a shot, despite her protestations. I went to her hammock, pulled her up, and turned her over. I wasn't prepared for what I saw. She was laying in her own diarrhea and there were about twenty long roundworms crawling all over her backside. This is the one and only time I yelled at an Indian.

"How long has she been like this?" I demanded of Felipe. "Why didn't you tell me it was parasites?"

I started to cry and began giving orders to her mother. Carlotta, little Carlotta who was named after Grandma Charlotte. Little Carlotta, who giggled all the time, who held up her arms for me to pick her up when I visited, little Carlotta who came often, yelling, "Vitamina, Carmelina." Now she lay dying, dying from roundworms.

Roundworms can cause havoc. They can work their way up the esophagus and get into the lungs, they can cause bowel obstructions, bloody noses, and brain damage; but they are treatable if caught early. Three little pills, an afternoon of stomach cramps. Six weeks later, a fol-low-up treatment. Three more little pills, an afternoon of very minor stomach cramps, and you're cured! Worm free! That people still die around the world from worms due to lack of education and medication appalls me. But to think precious Carlotta was dying before my eyes, under my care, was something I could not grasp.

"Oh, God, save her, heal her, please Lord. I love her," I prayed out loud, leaning over her hammock, holding her.

With her Mom's help, we cleaned her up. I tried to give her medica-tion and broth. She was too weak. Two days later the wailing started. The mournful, awful sound filled with agony that signals the death of a loved one. This also marked the death of any interest Felipe had in spiritual things. No longer did he preach, no more singing of hymns at 5:30 a.m. He rejected us, rejected everything we had to offer, rejected the limited knowledge he had of the gospel. He became hateful to us. He threatened our lives. He hired a witch doctor from another village to put a curse on us. He acted like a man possessed. He had been such a friendly, jolly person. Now he was sour, bitter, and angry—mourning the loss of Carlotta.

Pedro

Pedro was a little boy about eight years old—his family lived in the house right next door to us. He was such a cute little boy and we were used to seeing him run around the house, playing with his little bow and arrow, shooting grasshoppers, having a good time. He loved my girls and the girls loved him. They often played together.

One day his parents brought him to the porch. He was ill. They were vague about his symptoms. The people would get it in their heads that if something was serious, all they needed was a shot, and a shot would cure them. That's what Pedro's parents wanted. They weren't always honest about the symptoms nor were they very observant or educated about what to look for in a child's behavior as far as symptoms went. Pedro had a very high fever and Jack asked the father if it came and went in cycles and if he had chills.

"Oh, yes, yes, that's what he's got."

So we started him on a malaria treatment. Pedro didn't improve. A couple of days later they brought him back; he was looking terrible. We had to finish the malaria treatment because it's not a good thing to start treatment and then stop it. We didn't really know where to go from there. We had discussed his case with the doctor at the center over the radio—we still weren't getting much of a clue as to what was wrong. Two days later, we saw the parents dragging Pedro down the path toward our house. He had white foamy stuff coming out of his mouth and we asked, "What is that?"

"Oh, that's the medicine we got from across the river and he threw it up." There was now a new place across the river that gave drugs.

After hearing this, we didn't want to give him anything because we weren't sure what kind of medicine he had been given and we didn't want to mix drugs, and we sure didn't want to kill him with an overdose. We didn't know what to do. We did nothing. Late that night, they came for candles. A couple hours later, they came for more candles.

"How is he doing?"

"Bad, very bad."

We lay in bed and prayed. Jack decided to go sit with them. After Jack left, I couldn't sleep, so I just prayed. From our upper loft, lying in bed, I could almost touch the grass roof above my head. I heard a little rustling in this grass and I thought probably just a cockroach. In Colombia, cockroaches can be up to six inches long. I tried to disregard it and continued to pray; but the rustling persisted, and finally I grabbed my flashlight and shined it overhead. There, just above my head, about eighteen inches, was a very long snake.

I was petrified, paralyzed. Should I yell for Jack? I knew he was close enough. No, that would wake the girls and besides, the family was experiencing a tragedy. I carefully got up, dressed, and walked to the village. It was about one-thirty in the morning. To be polite, you don't just come rushing up and say, "Jack, there's a snake in the bedroom" You come up and say, "Hi, how is your little boy?" This custom often frustrated us. They would come to the porch and say, "Hi, how are you?" We would stand and chat; making small talk, being polite. "Oh by the way, I cut my foot," and you would look down and see lots of blood pouring out. Why didn't they just come out and tell us the purpose for the visit? Tonight, to honor their custom, I waited, wanting to be polite.

I waited as long as I felt I could. "Jack," I whispered, "there's a snake in the bedroom."

A few minutes later, Jack got up, excused himself, and walked to the house. I sat with the family. We didn't want to detract from the horrible fact that their little boy, little Pedro, was dying. By now, his abdomen was very swollen and he wasn't conscious. It was very sad. It was obvious they loved their children as much as we loved ours. Their losses are not lessened by the fact that many children do not survive childhood. Of course, my thoughts and prayers were for Jack too. I prayed he could find and kill the snake. In about forty-five minutes he returned, greeted everyone, and sat down. The snake was dead. We stayed for a while, and then walked home. We lay down with heavy hearts. About 4:00 a.m. the wailing started. Another beloved child had died.

Prince

Moises' oldest daughter, Glo, had gotten married and had given Moises
not only his first grandchild, but a boy at that. All were ecstatic. He was
treated like a prince, so that is what we called him—Prince. I don't think
his little feet touched the ground the first year of his life. He was chubby
and cute. By two years, he was toddling all over, charming everyone he
looked at. One day, his parents went to the river to fish and little Prince
was sitting on the shore among some reeds, splashing and having fun;
the large water moccasin struck Prince, sinking his fangs deep into his
chubby little leg. The young parents ran to the witch doctor, who "blew"
over him all night. "Blowing" smoke from a pipe over a sick person was
thought to chase away the evil spirits that were causing the sickness.

The following day, Prince was brought to us. His leg was swollen
almost as big as his trunk. He was feverish and in pain, moaning softly.
Moises and Mer were there, along with the parents. We gave an antivenin
injection, knowing it was probably too late. The shot made him cry, so
I rocked him in my lap for a while. He became quiet—I thought he was
asleep, but soon it became evident that he had died in my arms. The
wailing began.

People from the village came to our porch to see who had died. All
the women began to wail for Prince, for Moises's only grandson. We cried
along with them, "Lord, why? Three children in four weeks! Why?"

Mer, Moises' wife had never spoken to me—not in all the years we
lived in Macuare. I didn't know why. I thought she must not be a very
social person, as she didn't talk much even to the other women. This day,
the day of the death of her only grandchild, she sat huddled in a corner.
No sound came from her. No wailing. She sat in stony silence. I had
long since placed the dead child in his mother's arms, so I went over and
sat beside Mer. I put my arm around her. This gesture is not done in this
culture, but I couldn't help myself. I felt compelled somehow to let her
know I cared, to somehow let her know God cared. She turned toward

me, and a tear rolled down her cheek. She actually moved a little closer to me. No words were spoken. No words were needed.

Four more children died that summer; children we had grown to love. Words cannot describe how we felt as we climbed into the plane to return to Lomalinda. We had no answers for the people. We too, had only questions. We returned to Lomalinda with heavy hearts and began working on a hymnal.

17

BATS, BATS,
AND MORE BATS

"The Lord is my strength and my song;
he has become my salvation."

EXODUS 15:2

We were very sad, so very sad. We were truly mourning the death of so many precious children. Why had God allowed this to happen? What possible purpose was served? And now we were scheduled to work on hymnals? Songs of praise? I rebelled. I didn't want to work on hymnals. I didn't feel like working on songs of praise. To be perfectly honest, I didn't feel like praising a God who senselessly let seven children die.

How long God allowed this childish temper tantrum to last I don't recall. What I do recall is His tender voice wooing me, calling me, gently reminding me, *I loved those children more than you ever could, all things are not for you to understand, you are to trust and obey.* Slowly, I moved back toward my God and my Savior. I poured out my broken heart to Him and found comfort in His loving arms. Now, at last, I was able to begin work on the hymnals, the songs of praise.

The Wallers had already translated most of these hymns. We added a few more and knew that this collection would make a nice book for the Indians. For the cover, Jack being the artist that he was, drew a picture of a young Indian boy with a group of Indians behind him. They were all singing as in a choir. We chose red for the cover, as this was a favorite of the Indians. The print shop ran off one hundred copies for us and we brought them home and plopped them down in the kitchen. After dinner, we cleared every available space—the countertop, tabletop, set up chairs—and anything else we could think of to provide space for the pages of the book. Then, with the help of our girls and Taik Beniasa, a good friend, we began to collate the pages. The repetitive nature of hand collating soon became tedious, so we started singing and collated to the rhythm of our songs; these were hymnals, after all. One of the hymns we sang was *There is Joy in Serving Jesus*. Hours later, after we had stapled the pages together, stacked the finished products neatly in a corner ready for the cover to be glued on at the print shop the following day, and sent the girls to bed, we flopped down in the hammocks on the porch, relishing the joy of our accomplishment.

"There really is joy in serving Jesus," Jack said.

Taik and I nodded our agreement as we contently swayed in our hammocks.

We often took cooking pots, fabric, candles, matches, and machetes to Macuare and sold these to the Indians. They could buy these necessities on the barges that passed on the river close to the village, but the price was more than double what we charged, as we charged only our cost. Jack decided it would be a good idea to have a large supply of these items when we returned with the hymnals, so he planned a quick trip to Bogotá. He managed to fit on a flight going into the city, but had to take a bus back to Lomalinda. It was night. As a whole, Colombians are very emotive. On every international flight into Bogotá, they clap and cheer on landing. On bus trips over the mountains, they often screamed as we flew around a corner. This night, all was quiet except for one woman who had motion sickness and kept jumping up to vomit out her window. All at once she began screaming, "Parase! Parase! Stop the bus, stop the bus! My false teeth just fell out!"

The bus driver slammed on his brakes. Everyone piled out of the bus to look for the teeth. Jack prayed he wouldn't be the one to find the teeth.

"Aqui, aqui!"

A fellow passenger had found the valuable teeth; the woman wiped them off and stuck them back in her mouth. Everyone piled back into the bus and off they went, Jack being very grateful he hadn't found the missing teeth.

One of the marvelous benefits of living at Lomalinda was the fellowship of other believers. How we missed this in the village. On Wednesday nights, a prayer meeting was held on each *loma*. We liked to host this when we were there, so one Wednesday evening, several people were gathered in our living room. We shared the sad events of the deaths of so many children, our concern as to how this would affect our relationship with the people and finally, we asked that the hymnal would be well received. Many other requests were made and we entered into prayer. Prayer meetings with a bunch of missionaries are a wonderful experience. Everyone is eager to praise God and seek His help as we labor together. Sometimes these prayer meetings lasted several hours. This particular night however, was shorter than most. We hadn't been in reverent prayer long before we heard our neighbor JoAnn clearly say, "There's a bat on my shoulder!"

All heads popped up in unison and sure enough, there on her left shoulder perched a small bat. Immediately there ensued much shouting of advice, squeals, and scurryings around till finally the bat was captured. We settled down to the business of prayer again, but were unable to recapture the reverence. Each opening prayer was quickly interrupted by a snicker, which triggered another snicker. Snickering is contagious and soon, we just gave up, thanking God for knowing our needs even before we do, and closed the evening in praise.

We knew we had a bat problem at Lomalinda, as this wasn't the first bat that had managed to get into the house. Jack had designed our house to have a six-inch dead air space between the roof and the ceiling to provide insulation. This worked well for insulation, but unfortunately created a haven for bats.

Someone had told us that mothballs repel bats, so we bought several pounds of mothballs and poured them into the dead air space. Contrary to what we had been told, our bats seemed to like the mothballs and played with them, rolling them around over our heads.

Next, we decided the only solution would be to completely fill all the holes between the roof and the walls, sealing them up tight. Lee Hendrickson came to help Jack do this. They worked all afternoon, standing on scaffolding, moving it along as they worked their way to the peak of the roof. Bats have a pattern of leaving their dwelling place just at sundown. Our plan was to have most of the holes filled in, leaving only a few that would provide the escape for the bats at sundown, and then fill in the remaining holes as soon as the bats had vacated the place.

We had no idea the extent of the bat population in our attic. I figured ten to twenty. So you can imagine my shock at sundown as I watched from below, the guys high above my head, as hundreds of bats exited the few remaining holes, nearly knocking Lee and Jack off the scaffold. The guys ducked as they covered their heads with their arms. The exodus lasted ten to fifteen minutes. Hundreds and hundreds of bats swirled around before flying off to find food. When at last we were convinced the bats were all gone, Jack and Lee filled in the remaining holes and came off the scaffolding. There, that should do it! We were certain our bat problem had been taken care of.

We thanked Lee and I went in to fix supper. As I entered the house, I could hear squeaks and squeals. I guessed there must have been some bats that were trapped in the dead air space. Would they die trapped in there? If so, how long would take? And how much would it smell if they did die up there?

We ate supper and then the real fun began. The bats had found a way into the house and one by one were entering the living room. Well, I guess that was better than them dying in the dead air space. There were several young men in the center that had snakes and we knew the snakes liked warm meat; warm bat meat would do just fine for a delightful meal for many snakes. We used a tennis racket to hit the bats, stunning them until we could put them into a glass jar. That first night, we collected fifty-eight bats. My arm was sore from hitting at them with the tennis racket. The second night we collected forty-seven more bats. The third night netted only eighteen bats and by the fourth night, the nine remaining bats were dehydrated and easily caught. One hundred thirty-two bats in all. All the snakes in the center were stuffed and wouldn't eat again for days, maybe weeks. Their owners didn't want any more live, warm food. As for us, on the fifth night, we ate an early supper, manned our positions, took up our tennis rackets, and waited. The silence seemed eerie. Thirty minutes past dusk and no sign of bats. An hour passed, and still no sound, no bat. Was it possible the bats were finally gone? Well, praise the Lord! This solution proved to be permanent, as we never had another bat in the house.

18

THE PEACE OFFERING

///

"We love because He first loved us."

I John 4:19

The problem of the bats solved, we once again turned our attention to the tribe. We scheduled a flight to take us back to Macuare. It had been almost six months since we had been there. We wondered how our reception would be. Would they hold us responsible for the deaths of the children? Would the trust we had managed to gain be gone?

We packed up all the merchandise bought in Bogotá, the hymnals and our personal supplies, and headed to the village. As always, the people gathered around the plane, grabbed all our stuff, and ran off to the house with everything. We unpacked the hymnals while they were still sitting, scattered all over the porch. Felipe was there and he looked at the book and said, "Ah, these are nice, give me ten."

Jack said, "Well, we're not going to give these away. They're for sale. They'll cost ten pesos a piece."

That's about twenty-five cents. We had prayed about this because this would be the first time we had sold anything. We usually just gave away copies, so the people were used to that. When we prayed about it, we first decided on twenty pesos. But when we were in the plane coming out, Jack asked, "How about ten?" I quickly agreed.

We were hoping that this would make these little books mean more to the people if they had to pay a little something for them. As soon as Felipe found out they were ten pesos, he didn't want any and started yelling, "I'm a better Christian than you are. You're supposed to be a big missionary, a big evangelical. You're supposed to give me things! I give you fish all the time. I give you this land to build your house, and who are you to come here and tell me how to live? You come here and charge me ten pesos for this book."

In his anger, he stomped off the porch and marched down the trail. Felipe was the chief and everyone's boss, so no one else dared to buy a book.

The next day, there was another group of people visiting from another village. One of these men stepped up and told Jack that he'd like to buy one of the hymnals. Felipe sat there and began to make fun of him, yelling, "That book is full of lies. It won't do any good. We believed that way, our crops failed, and my little girl Carlotta died."

It was difficult to live in the village with him because of the continuous conflict, day after day. Quite often he wouldn't go to his field because he didn't want to be close even to the other Indians, so they would go out to the fields without him. We were wondering how God was going to handle this situation. Things seemed to be in a stalemate.

In March, the kids had a week off for Spring Break and we were all six at Macuare. This was during the dry season, and one day, there were only two other families in the village. Felipe and his family were gone fishing. His cocoa fields caught on fire and a man ran to our house and said, "Oh, you know Felipe's cocoa fields are on fire!"

Jack said, "Well, go and tell him and his family."

"No, they've all gone fishing."

Jack said, "Well, how about you? Will you help put it out?"

And the man said, "No, he's not my brother. I have absolutely no responsibility."

So, Jack, Kerry, Lorrie, Joy, and I spent the rest of the day fighting the fire alone. It was located halfway to the stream, and our girls carried buckets of water on their heads all day. Jack and I were at the fire with hoes and machetes. It was about 120 degrees near the fires. While we managed to get the fire out and saved most of the field, Felipe still lost about ten trees. That night, we collapsed on the porch, and Kerry said, "I hope Felipe comes over here tonight when he gets home from his fishing trip and says a great big, 'Thank you'."

This gave us another opportunity to talk to our children about why we do what we do. Felipe would probably not say thank you. For one thing, they don't have a word for thank you in their language and they don't feel gratitude. They haven't been taught to feel gratitude. If you did something nice for someone else, then they would owe you a favor and they might be mad you had indebted them to you.

However, we didn't do these things for gratitude, but for the Lord, whether anybody was thankful or not, and we had to keep that in mind. So far, no one here had been thankful for anything we had done.

The next morning, Felipe returned from his fishing trip and was informed of all the events of the weekend and the part we had played. He walked over to our house with a huge gourd full of purple, milky, *koo* juice. It was kind of yucky. He also had several small gourds, and these he handed to us. He had us all sit down and he poured each of us a gourd full of *koo* juice. This was his way of saying thanks. It was very meaningful to us—we had done something for him out of love—to show him love—in spite of the fact that he had rejected us, threatened to kill us, and tried to get rid of us, we had continued to love him. After his offering of *koo* juice, his attitude toward us mellowed. He was still not as friendly as he once had been, but still, it was a great improvement. I'm sure he was grieving the loss of little Carlotta.

19

CHET HAS BEEN SHOT

*"Get rid of all bitterness, rage, and anger...
forgiving each other, just as in Christ God forgave you."*

EPHESIANS 4:31, 32

Once again, we returned to Lomalinda. Back at the base, our thoughts quickly turned to computers. Our branch had the opportunity to buy several computers, each translator personally paying for their own. The main office was sending a man to instruct us on how to use these wonderful new machines. The computer course was six weeks long. For translating, publishing, and making dictionaries, etc., these would save hours and hours, plus be more accurate. A new building, the Technical Studies Department (TSD), had been built to house the computers. Each translator had a small cubicle. Best of all, it was air-conditioned! This was to protect the equipment from dust, humidity, and heat. The translators loved it.

The day we finished the course, we were given certificates. There was cake, coffee, and much gaiety. We were all very excited to start entering our own data. I drove home on my motorcycle to fix lunch, dreaming of working in an air-conditioned building later that afternoon. I looked up and saw Chet Bitterman coming right at me. He was driving on my side of the road. He was staring off to his left, not paying attention and driving very fast. At the last moment, I decided to swerve into his lane so we could pass each other on the wrong side. Unfortunately, he looked up just as I pulled into his lane and automatically pulled his motorcycle into his proper lane, and we crashed. His front tire caught my back tire. I went flying over the handlebars and landed with a thud. I was hurt and I knew it. I glanced over at my bike. It was mangled. Chet leaned over me.

"Are you all right? I'm so sorry. Let me go get a vehicle."

I lay in the dirt. As I later discovered, my left knee was dislocated and my right wrist was broken. This meant a trip to Bogotá. It was too late that day, so we had to wait until the next day. The pain was awful. My arm was put in a cast that extended from my fingertips to my armpit. I was to wear this for six months, as little bones in the wrist are not really set in the traditional manner. No computers for me. My anger at Chet burned. I thought, *He was always driving like an idiot, way too fast.*

Jack, too, was angry with Chet. It was awkward. We lived in a very small center. Chet and his wife, Brenda, avoided us, and we avoided them. This went on for about a month. Jack decided to go to the tribe alone, as I could not very well go with this large cast. We sat in our living room and pondered the situation.

Macuare is very dark. This is difficult to describe. It is not a place I would want to be in if I wasn't right with God and man. We decided that we needed to get this issue with Chet and Brenda resolved. We called them and arranged to visit them at their house after church the following Sunday night. I told them I had been very angry and I asked them to forgive me. Jack too, told them he had been very angry and asked them to forgive him. Chet asked our forgiveness for driving so carelessly. What powerful words. What joy to be restored and reconciled with a brother. We all cried and hugged. Then we prayed together. Now, we felt, Jack was prepared to go to the tribe alone.

My mother and sister Kay had heard discouragement in my letters and decided to pay me a visit. They could also help me, as the cast limited my abilities to cook and clean. They flew into Bogotá and spent one night at the group house. My good friend, Ivy Tattersoll, lived in Bogotá and made arrangements for them to come to Lomalinda. Chet happened to be in Bogotá the night they were there and they met him. Later, in Lomalinda, I told Mom and Kay that it was Chet who had run into me, and Kay exclaimed, "I'll just give that young man a piece of my mind if he's still there when we go back!"

I pleaded with her not to do that, that we had just worked things out with Chet and Brenda and wanted them to stay that way.

"Okay," she said, "but I just wish I could teach him a lesson."

On January 19, 1981, just two days later, several masked guerillas broke into the Group House just before dawn and gathered everyone in the dining room. They made all the missionaries lie facedown and tied them up. For some reason, they decided to take Chet. We got the news first thing that morning. Chet had been kidnapped.

Kay and Mother were frightened and decided to shorten their visit. They wanted to return to the United States immediately. In Bogotá, they stayed with Norm and Ivy instead of the Group House. We were glad to hear they arrived home safely.

Four days later, on January 23, my birthday, the guerillas, a group called M-19 (the Movement of April Nineteenth) made their demands.

There were two conditions:

1. Removal from Colombia of the entire organization of WBT by February 19.

2. Publish a document they would send to us in the *Washington Post* and the *New York Times*.

If we didn't comply, Chet would be shot. All personnel were to leave. We were to leave all our possessions behind. It was signed

M-19

Win or Die

Three weeks. We had been given only three weeks to leave Colombia. Jack was on the Executive Committee and they called a special meeting. Jack called me from the meeting.

"There was really no decision to make. There is only one thing to do."

"Yes," I agreed and started thinking what things we would take. I told the girls they could each take two things.

Kerry loved her flute, but had a beloved stuffed monkey she'd had since her birth. She also had a long thick braid that she had saved when she cut her hair. Her flute would have to stay.

Lorrie decided she would take her school album and...Kerry's flute.

Joy, of course, wanted to take her collection of turtles. She had two parents and two children. She struggled with which two she would leave behind, the parents or the babies? Finally, as her lower lip quivered, she stated, "I'll take the parents."

Seven-year-old Janey, without a moment's hesitation, popped out, "I'll take Joy's turtle children!"

I thought, what clothes would we need? Just enough to get us by. We could always buy things once in the States.

That night Jack came home for supper and we told him all we decided. He looked at me, disbelieving. "What do you mean? We're not going anyplace!"

"I thought you said there was really only one thing we could do."

"I did! We have to stay. We won't negotiate with subversive groups! We all signed contracts, remember? If we were ever kidnapped, no ransom would be paid. No negotiations made. Don't you remember this?"

Yes, yes I knew that, but that was theory, this was real! I was stunned. Brenda and her two little girls flew to the United States. Jack went to Bogotá to help talk with government officials. Chet's parents came to Lomalinda and spoke to us. They told us Chet had loved the verse in Philippians, "I want to know Christ and the power of his resurrection and the fellowship of sharing in his sufferings, becoming like him in his death" (Philippians 3:10). They shared an entry from Chet's diary:

Costa Rica, September 1978. "The situation in Nicaragua is getting worse. If Nicaragua falls, I guess the rest of Central America will too. Maybe this is just some kind of self inflicted martyr complex, but I find this recurring thought that perhaps God will call me to be martyred for Him in His Service in Colombia. I am willing."

Chet had shared with his parents that he felt strongly God would use him somehow. They concluded that maybe Chet had been born for such a time as this. Chet told Brenda, "Some trust in chariots and some in horses, but we trust in the name of the Lord our God (Psalms 20:7). Be strong!"

The next three weeks were tense. The Colombian government moved troops to live in and around the center to protect us. A curfew was imposed; no one, under any circumstances, was to be out after dark. The Colombian branch set up a twenty-four hour prayer vigil. Christians around the world were called on to pray and pray they did.

The morning the phone rang, I knew, somehow, I just knew. My worst fears materialized. "Chet has been shot in the heart on a bus. He died instantly." A new truth hit me. You could die trusting the Lord.

Many years ago, I had made a decision; I was willing to live for the Lord. Now, I had to make another decision. Was I also willing to die for the Lord? I thought about this the rest of the day. We gathered in the auditorium to pray—for Brenda, her little girls, Chet's parents, for the kidnappers, for ourselves, the work in Colombia, God's direction, God's comfort. Sometime during that prayer meeting, I said, "Yes, Lord, yes. I am willing to die for You. If that is what You want, then I am willing. Not my will, but Yours."

The peace that comes with complete surrender washed over me. Trusting in a loving Father gives us freedom to live without fear or regrets. Trusting in a loving Father gives us the freedom to live in joy no matter what happens.

I thought about Chet. I thought about being so angry with him for running into me on his motorcycle. I thought about the night we went to his house to make amends. I knew God prompted us to do that. God knew that Chet's days were numbered. God knew that I wouldn't have been able to carry an unresolved burden for the rest of my life. What a valuable lesson I learned. What a loving Father we have. The Bible says not to let the sun go down on your anger. We need to be quick to forgive, quick to resolve issues with others. We never know what tomorrow will bring.

Things were never quite the same at Lomalinda after Chet's murder. The army stayed for several months. We had threats over the radio that more *gringos* would be kidnapped and killed. Some families left the country.

At one point, I had to take Kerry and Lorrie into Bogotá because of a visa problem. We got to the city, did our business, and headed straight back to the center. Our planes were busy flying translators in and out of their tribes, so we chartered a flight out of Villavicencio. The two young pilots seemed friendly enough. We climbed aboard, strapped ourselves in, and started taxiing down the runway. I asked God for protection and a safe flight. This is usually a short thirty-minute flight. When we had been airborne forty-five minutes, I began to get anxious. Kerry and Lorrie were also trying very hard not to panic. Were we being kidnapped? The two men were talking and pointing out the window. They looked as nervous as we did. Finally, I tapped one on his shoulder and said, "We should have been there by now."

"Sí, Sí, Señora, we are lost!"

In any other circumstance, those words wouldn't have been welcome, but today, I wanted to shout Praise the Lord! Hallelujah! We're not being kidnapped! We're just lost! I'd made this trip hundreds of times. This was their first. I looked out the window at the river below. Way back to the left, I could just barely see Puerto Lleras at the bend of the San Jose del Guaviare River. I told our pilots to turn around and follow the river. They did, and very soon Lomalinda came into view. The two men were smiling now, animated. It had been one hour and fifteen minutes since we left Villavicencio. These pilots had radioed when we took off, so all of Lomalinda knew we were in trouble and, of course, everyone assumed the worse. The crowd that had gathered clapped and cheered when we disembarked. We were welcomed home like celebrities.

No, things at Lomalinda were never the same following Chet's murder. The carefree lifestyle was replaced by fear. Fear of a stranger walking around the base. Fear even of the soldiers the government had sent to protect us. Most were young boys aged between sixteen and eighteen and were careless with the rifles they carried. One shot himself in the foot. Another shot a follow soldier in the shoulder. I didn't trust them with my beautiful young daughters, so I required they have a buddy system and no longer wander around alone. We took what precautions we could and left the rest in the hands of God.

20

A BAND OF GUERILLAS

"I know that everything God does will endure forever;
nothing can be added to it and nothing taken from it."

ECCLESIASTES 3:14

*D*espite all this political unrest, we decided to visit the tribe again. I was somewhat nervous, but this was what we came to do. Jack had completed *The Life of Christ* and was working on the *Old Testament Summary*. I was working on primers. I had held a few literacy classes with some of the children the last time we were in the tribe, had made some changes, and wanted to test these. We stayed six weeks, finished our checking, and packed up. Unknown to us, a band of guerillas was close by at the river. As Tom Smoak circled in and landed, they heard the plane and came to the village. For the next four hours, they held us at gunpoint. They had machine guns. There were eight of them. The kids were pretty calm. They had a little red tape recorder and the guerillas took that. That upset them more than the guns. "We'll buy you another," I reassured them.

We had sprinkled insect repellant around the poles of our house to discourage termites. The men continued to taste this powder, thinking maybe it was drugs. More than once they asked, "What is this stuff?" I told them it was poison. Finally, this man who stood only a couple of feet from me realized I was telling the truth, and in fact it was poison. As the realization of this hit him, he promptly spit it all over my face! *Okay, this is not going to make me mad—you have the machine gun.*

"Go get me water," he ordered me.

I ran to the well. We both washed off. I remained remarkably calm. We had just finished reading *The Silver Chair* by C.S. Lewis. This wonderful book from *The Chronicles of Narnia* series is about obedience. Two children and a Marshwiggle are given four signs. They muff the first three signs. Finally, for the last sign, they are to do whatever is asked if it is asked in the name of Aslan. The circumstances appear that if they actually do this thing, they will all be killed. They choose to obey. Whether we live or die, Aslan is still our good Lord...

This day in the jungle, being held at gunpoint, I too, thought, *Whether I live or die, Jesus is still my good Lord.* I had wrestled this out in my mind many months before. Now, I pictured Jesus as a huge lion, walking just a short distance from us in the tall grasses, there to save us, or maybe to take us to heaven.

For some reason, we were released and allowed to return to the center. My calm while in the situation disappeared in the plane. Hebrews 4:16 came to mind—"Let us then approach the throne of grace with confidence, so that we may receive mercy and find grace to help, help, help...." I started to shake. I could not stop shaking, all the way to Lomalinda I shook. I didn't know it then, but I was never to return to Macuare.

We later learned the men destroyed our house, the outhouse, and the office. They burned fields, destroying all the crops, but by far the worst of it was the killing of two Indians. Finally, they threatened if we ever came back, more Indians would be killed and—we, too, would be killed. There was nothing left. Nothing. No physical evidence that we had ever lived at Macuare. While it is true these guerillas eradicated all physical evidence of our many years in this village, I was comforted knowing the things God had accomplished here belonged in a realm far above what the guerillas could touch, and thus would endure forever.

We had worked in this tribe almost seventeen years. We had very little to show for all those years. We had *The Life of Christ*, a hymnal, some primers, and a handful of readers. Some of our friends had hundreds of believers, enough of them industrious readers that they not only read themselves, but had even organized classes for their entire tribe. We had no believers, no response whatsoever.

A friend of ours had been kidnapped and killed. A friend from another mission had also been kidnapped, but had escaped. An American couple we knew had been kidnapped. Jack was discouraged. Disillusioned. Frustrated. Many times I reminded him, "We are called to obedience, not success." This didn't help. He was angry and depressed. We needed some time off. We needed some help. Kerry and Lorrie were now in high school and we decided this was a good time for a furlough.

21

JACK

"He that thinks he stands, take heed, lest he fall."
1 CORINTHIANS 10:12 KJV

Circumstances in life can bombard us, cause experiences of doubt, disillusionment, hurt, and pain. We decide how we will deal with those circumstances. We always have a choice, and how we choose will make a difference as to how we will survive catastrophes or problems that sometimes are far beyond our control.

The next few years were painful. Our marriage began to unravel. We went for counseling, but nothing seemed to help. We were on a downhill slope, quickly careening toward destruction. Jack began drinking heavily. He was extremely depressed. He often stayed out late at night, and I didn't know where he was.

One night, the police called me to come and pick him up; he had been stabbed in the groin. He couldn't drive, but wasn't seriously hurt and didn't want to go the hospital. Joy and Janey were asleep in their beds. In the middle of the night, I drove down to the red light district of Dallas to get him. We didn't speak on the trip back home.

Shortly after this incident, I filed for divorce. Several Wycliffe friends reminded me that God hates divorce. I, too, hate divorce. In our human frailty, when a marriage takes place, it is like two sheets of tissue paper glued together becoming one. If divorce occurs, you attempt to pull apart these tissues, leaving only a pile of tiny shreds. No, I didn't need to be reminded that God hates divorce, that divorce was never part of His plan for us, His beloved children.

Nor did I feel the need or desire to defend my actions. Deep within the chambers of my broken heart, I still clung to the hope that God would answer my prayers that Jack would return to his senses, that we would be reunited, reconciled, and return to Macuare and finish our work. My rationale being that when this happened, the fewer people who knew the depths of the problem, the easier it would be to return to "normal." Thus, my actions minus an explanation led Wycliffe to request my resignation. As I wrote the letter, my mind drifted back to the little church in Lubbock so many years ago when God had first called to me. When God first made it known that I was to become a missionary. My old misconception that missionaries lived happily ever after was now as shattered as my heart. The letter lay on my desk for many days. Finally, on one of the saddest days of my life, with a heavy, heavy heart, I mailed the letter resigning from Wycliffe.

I was no longer a missionary. Soon, I would no longer be a wife. These were titles that defined me. Who was I now? How close, how precious was the Spirit of God during these days as I leaned on Him for strength. I was simply a child of God, one of His little lambs. He was my Shepherd and He would once again lead me beside still waters. He would comfort me with His Word.

"I have summoned you by name, you are mine. When you pass through the waters, I will be with you; and when you pass through the rivers, they will not sweep over you. When you walk through the fire, you will not be burned; the flames will not set you ablaze. For I am the Lord, your God" (Isaiah 43:1–3).

Joy, Janey, and I moved into an apartment. Jack remained in Wycliffe less than a year. He sold our house and moved to Lubbock into the room above the print shop owned by his father. This didn't last long. He then went to live a while with Kerry; soon Lorrie got him a job, so he went to Tennessee and moved in with her. This new job lasted less than a day.

In the end, the depression won. On June 29, 1993, Jack took his own life.

Suicide is something you never get over. You never recover. You just survive. You go on. You learn to live with it. Life is for the living. You begin living. You resume going to your job, you resume eating, sleeping, watching TV, and complaining about the weather. You take on the appearance of normalcy. Then a grandchild is born. Such a joyous occasion, but wham, it hits you in the gut. Where is the grandfather? Oh yes, he checked out. How could he choose not to be here? What pain of his could possibly have been greater than this joy? College graduations, family reunions, a beautiful sunset, and a thousand other little bits of life remind you of this moment, this moment a person chose to end his life.

I knew my pain was enormous. I also knew the pain my daughters felt was far greater than my own. I had to be strong for them. I would cling to God as never before. I would lead the way out of this dark jungle by my example. "Through many dangers, toils, and snares I have already come." I would try to comfort them as best as I could. I would try to help them understand something none of us would ever understand. In the months following Jack's death, I tormented myself with a desire to understand how this had happened.

Oh Jack, beloved of my youth, what were you thinking? Did you forget God called us to do a great work for Him? Did you forget our combined joy the day Vicente announced he would help us learn the language? Did you forget the joy of making stilts with the Indians or the fun we had watching them play with ice? Did you forget the look on the faces of the young boys as they learned to read? Did you forget swinging in our hammocks on a Sunday afternoon, listening to a football game via short wave radio and laughing as the Indians all cheered with us as our team scored, even though they had no clue what it was all about? Did you forget the wonderful times we had with our own children in the evenings, alone, just our family, reading, singing, and praying together? Did you forget the tiny green tree frog that landed on Joy and all six of us bounced around on the bunk beds trying to catch him, laughing hysterically? Did you forget walking ten miles round trip just to give an old lady a shot? Did you forget there is joy in serving Jesus? Did you forget that your youngest grandchild wasn't even two months old yet? Did you forget Joy was pregnant with another wonderful grandchild? Did you forget His grace is sufficient?

You have missed so much I don't even know where to start. Kerry did go into computers for a while as she planned, but then decided the corporate world wasn't for her and went back to school and became a chef. This didn't surprise me, as she was so often in the kitchen with me, cooking this or that. Remember the Christmas at Lomalinda when Kerry and Lorrie made Julekake for about twenty families? The little balls of dough forming Christmas trees then decorated accordingly? No, it's no surprise she is a chef.

Do you remember the night the three of us spent in Villavicencio? The ugly little room we found vacant in that cheap little hotel in the middle of town, the bar across the street playing music late into the night, the toilet sitting in the corner with only a thin curtain for privacy, the three little cots, side by side where we tried to sleep and Kerry stating in the darkness, "I will *never* be a missionary!" For a while following your death, she claimed she would never darken the doors of a church again, but God has been faithful. She is currently serving as a missionary in Cameroon with Wycliffe Associates. You would be so proud.

Lorrie has become a Math teacher. What a time we had teaching her fractions in the tribe. Do you remember the day I finally thought I'd gotten the concept through to her cute little head and I asked her if I made a lemon pie, would she rather have 1/4 or 1/8 and she replied 1/8 and in my frustration I slammed my hand down on the table and shouted,

"Lorrie, why can't you get this?" To which she answered quietly,

"I'm not very hungry"

Oh, how we laughed! And now, to think she is a Math teacher imparting this exact science to so many little minds.

She has two wonderful sons. As a single mom, she has had much on her plate, but she has done a great job. You've missed out not knowing these wonderful young boys, soon to be young men. You would be so proud.

Joy is a beautiful young woman. Remember the constant daydreaming? The turtles? The imaginary friend Mayonnaise? Remember Mr. Zeckiel's Science class we thought Joy would never pass and the wonderful project you helped her build? No, she didn't grow up to be a scientist. She teaches World Geography in high school. The day she graduated from college was so bittersweet. I was immensely proud of her, but couldn't help but wish you were there. Knowing you, tears would have spilled. You would have been so proud.

Joy's three children are all so unique. These are sweet, thoughtful, delightful children. Do you remember David, Joy's high school sweetheart? Well, Jack, they are happily married now. God has been so faithful.

All four of your precious daughters have had years of struggles, years when they lost traction and just floundered. Janey has been the last to find her way. She's on course now and, God willing, she, too, will reach her goals. After numerous miscarriages, Jane and Todd are now the parents of a tiny little daughter, a premature angel. They are wonderful parents and their baby was less than two weeks old when they first took her to church. You would be so proud. And, oh yes, she wants to be called Jane now.

They have had it rough, Jack, forced to question their faith, their God, everything we taught them. So many tears, so much pain. They will never get over your death. They have just learned to live with it. Your grandchildren call you Papa Jack and remain like the rest of us, bewildered at your absence.

No, my dear, the depths of your torment I will never know, never understand. One beautiful summer morning, I stood in my kitchen and demanded, "God, I want to understand this!"

Remember the verses inscribed in your toolbox? The one Ed gave you? We memorized them and quoted them to each other often, "Trust in the Lord with all your heart and lean not on your own understanding; in all you ways acknowledge him, and he will direct your path" (Proverbs 3:5, 6).

We loved thinking of God directing our path. This morning, however, God directed my thinking to the line that says, "Lean not on your own understanding." It was as if God were saying to me, *"Carol, I understand, you don't have to."*

"But Lord," I argued, "I want to understand!"

"You don't need to, just trust and obey. I understand, that is enough."

So Jack, that morning, I gave up the need to understand this. Giving this up helped me to let go of some of the anger I held toward you. That morning I felt freer, lighter. A burden was lifted. Granted, there was still some anger burning inside me. How could you do this to your children? You pulled out the foundation from all four of them. You took the easy way out, insuring their way would be anything but easy. But miraculously, over the years, the anger I felt toward you has dissipated. Many times I prayed that God would give me the grace to forgive you and God is faithful. I do forgive you. No, I will never understand why you did what you did, but I am at peace with it. I trust that you, too, are at peace.

22

A NEW LIFE, A NEW LOVE

"Now to him who is able to do immeasurably more
than all we ask or imagine, according to his power
that is at work within us, to him be glory in the
church and in Christ Jesus throughout
all generations, for ever and ever!"

EPHESIANS 3:20

The years following that sad event have been filled to overflowing. God has done and continues to do exceedingly more than all I could have asked or imagined. Long ago, Kay and Roger moved to Dallas and now lived close to me. One fall, they began taking a six-month class in leadership at their church. Kay was very excited the morning she called to inform me there was a single man in the class. Over the next several months, I heard all about Dwight Martin, his commitment to God, his comments in the class, his profession, his daughter, Melissa, even the time when he had the flu. He didn't know I even existed. As the course was quickly coming to a close, Kay realized some action must be taken. She invited Dwight and me both over to dinner. After this initial meeting, we tentatively began to date. What a nice looking man. What a great sense of humor. How kind and thoughtful he was. Was it really possible that I was falling in love again? Yes, it appears that is just what was happening. Within a year Dwight and I were married. Thank you, Lord, for your kindness, for your faithfulness, for your provision of a companion.

We are now retired, but once a missionary, always a missionary, so we joined a ministry called SOWERS—Servants On Wheels Ever Ready. This is an RV ministry and we volunteer and work projects all over the United States, traveling and living in our motor home. What a privilege that we can still serve God. We have worked with and for many of God's most faithful servants.

We have also been privileged to support Vic and Riena Kondo, the missionaries that took up the work of the Guayaberos. The morning I began work on this chapter, I received an email from Riena. She wrote that she had just received a request for the little red hymnal. As there are only two copies left, they photocopied some to pass along. There are fifteen baptized believers and ten more being discipled. Thanks to their faithfulness, the Guayabero Scriptures are almost complete and will soon be published. I can picture the great multitude now. A multitude so big no one can count. A multitude including people from every nation, every tribe, and yes, even some Guayaberos.